Knowing the Unknown - I

Mysteries of Life - Past, Present, and Future

Manohar Lal, Ph.D.

Library of Congress Catalog Number: 2010931473
ISBN: 978-0-9826809-0-2

MRLT, LLC, Tulsa
Printed in the United States of America

Table of Contents

Preface

Acknowledgments

This is the first book in the series entitled Knowing the Unknown. It addresses the question; *"Who am I?"* It is a question that all of us ask frequently. The second book in this series, Mysteries of the Universe, addresses the question; *"Where am I?"* The third book in the series, Challenges of Technology, addresses the question, *"What am I doing?"*

I want to gratefully acknowledge the help that I received from all sources, which are too numerous to list. I have attempted to acknowledge and list the names of all the distinguished persons in this book who have contributed directly or indirectly in some manner. With the popularity of the Internet, one can easily find further information about their work by typing a few words on a search engine.

I also want to acknowledge the help received from my daughter-in-law, Ritu, who designed the cover page and helped me with pictures in the book. It would not have been possible to write this book if my friends, my children, my grandchildren, and my wife had not inspired me to do so. I would like to dedicate this book to all of them.

Preface

In this first book in the Knowing the Unknown series, the question, "Who am I" is addressed. The reader is taken on an exciting journey that unfolds into a panoramic view of life, providing a unique perspective on the origin, historical evolution, current frontiers, and the future of life. In this context, we also discuss the answers that science and religion present regarding the meaning, origin, and evolution of life. Our journey through life reveals that we do not really understand the true meaning of life. The question, "Who am I" still cannot fully be answered. While searching for the ultimate truth, the top ten mysteries of life are reviewed, and the very future of life is predicted.

This book also examines the questions that often arise as one goes through different stages of life. For example, the following questions concerning life are often asked: What is life? How did life begin? "Did 'outside' intelligence play a role? Did human life evolve or did some superpower create it? Does the notion of inner soul exist? Does God exist? All of these questions are discussed in an unbiased manner.

This is not just another book on life. It takes a detailed, objective look at the complexities of life from the perspectives of scientific theories and religions., As it attempts to explain the meaning of life, it brings together the most recent research and observations, raises further questions, explores its frontiers, and searches for the ultimate truth. The book should inspire the reader to appreciate the elegance, beauty, and complexity of life through understanding the true meaning behind the journey of life and its role in the universe.

This book contains my individual perspective on life. Whilst I am certainly not an 'expert' on all of the topics covered in this book, my unique perspective essentially comes from my diverse educational and professional background, personal experiences, and my eastern outlook, which combined together, motivated me to write this book . I hope that you, the reader, enjoy this journey as much as I have enjoyed writing it.

Manohar Lal, Ph.D.

.

Chapter 1
Origin & Journey of Humans

1.1 Introduction

The origin of life, its evolution, and our appearance on this planet were remarkable events. Science or religion has yet to explain these events completely. To search for the answers, we must go back in time to when humans first appeared on this planet and, based on the available evidence, trace humans' journey to the present age, before delving further back in time to the era of life before humans.

1.2 Journey to the Present

Let us visualize the time when humans first appeared on this planet. Let us analyze feelings, emotions, and reactions, as the first humans look around and find themselves surrounded by nature, wild beasts, trees, rivers, etc. Primitive humans are quite afraid and confused and do not understand the events happening around them. At this stage, the brain is not fully developed and, therefore, immediate concerns are personal security and survival. Humans instinctively try to protect themselves from the wild beasts and unfriendly forces of nature. Even today, these instincts exist.

As humans continue their journey, they learn to climb trees, build crude weapons from wood and stone, and ignite fires to scare the wild animals away. Gradually, they learn to hunt, control the environment, domesticate some animals, and grow food. This journey of man spans thousands of years. The key to survival and control of the environment lies in observing, collecting data, processing the observed data, learning, storing, and sharing the information. During this journey, various religions also come into existence, which prosper in different parts of the world. Let us trace this journey from the time man that appears on this planet.

A fascinating picture of the journey of man emerges, based on archaeological and genetic studies. Fig. 1.1 shows the timeline of the origin and journey of humanity to the present day.

Timeline for Mankind Journey	
~2,500,000	Homo erg aster appears in Africa, cradle of humanity
~1,500,000:	Homo erectus appears in Africa and expands to Eurasia
~ 500,000:	Homo erectus uses stone hand axes, and other tools for hunting
~ 300,000:	Neanderthals appear with better brain and vocal chords
~ 75,000	Last ice age begins
~ 50,000	Cro-Magnon – our ancestors appears, with superior brains
~ 40,000:	Our ancestors travel and, spread into Central Asia
~ 20,000:	Separated Asian populations reach, Europe through Russia
~ 15,000:	They cross over to North America, via Bering Sea and spread
~ 10,000	Last ice age ends after 65,000 yrs, population 4 million
0	Human beings roam planet earth, population over 6 billion

Fig. 1.1—Timeline for Human Origin & Journey

Evidence indicates that the African continent is the cradle of humanity, with East Africa noted as the specific place where Homo sapiens originated over 2.5 million years ago. Homo ergasters existed around 1.8 million years ago. They tried to survive as scavengers, eating whatever wild beasts left behind. Gradually, they learnt to use crude stone tools. Some members of this ancient human species started moving northwards, chasing additional food sources. Excavated remains indicate that they were living in Kenya around 1.6 million years ago.

Then, the Homo erectus—successor to the Homo ergaster species—appeared on the scene. There is consensus that Homo erectus, the precursor to modern humans, also evolved in Africa and gradually expanded to Eurasia approximately 1.7 million years ago. Archaeological evidence confirms they existed 300,000 years ago. The Homo erectus lineage refined stone tools, used spears and fire, hunted rather than being hunted, and ultimately rose higher in the food chain.

However, 100,000—50,000 years ago Homo erectus started to disappear. Homo sapiens replaced them and became the prominent species. How it happened still remains a mystery. The evidence suggests that around 100,000 years ago several species of hominids populated the Earth, including Homo sapiens in Africa, Homo erectus in South East Asia and China, and Neanderthals in Europe.

Neanderthals lived in freestanding settlements and caves and their brains were slightly more developed. They had better-crafted tools and lived in small groups in caves. Evidence also suggests that they developed vocal chords, essential for some kind of speech. They buried their dead with artifacts, thus indicating abstract thought and belief in an after-life. Their tools were more sophisticated, with handles to gain extra advantage. The Neanderthals, however, also became extinct. Nevertheless, these extinct humans were our closest relatives.

The Cro-Magnon lineage followed the Neanderthals. Their brains were more developed and because they were far superior hunters with light and sharp spears, they learnt to survive and adapt effectively to their environment. Homo ergaster, Homo erectus, and Neanderthals disappeared from the scene as they failed to survive.

According to Klein, an anthropologist at Stanford University, Homo sapiens may have had the anatomy of modern man as far back as 150,000 years ago. However, they become behaviorally modern only about 50,000 years ago. At that point, a genetic mutation related to cognition occurred, which made them more intelligent. According to Klein, this change in thinking ability enabled humans to construct sophisticated tools, build permanent lodgings, hunt more effectively, and possibly develop language. As a result, travel increased around that period. Additional reasons for migration could be increase in population, consumption of more meat and fish, and climate change.

According to the 'Out of Africa' theory, modern humans (Homo sapiens) evolved in East Africa. They then spread out across the globe, replacing earlier or archaic human populations such as the Neanderthals, with very little, if any, interbreeding. The dispersal of modern humans most probably began between 60,000 and 50,000 years ago, as an exodus from Africa began around this period.

From a 2010 analysis of Neanderthals genome, it was concluded that 1% and 4% of the Eurasian human genome seems to come from Neanderthals. Though the Neanderthal genetic contribution—found in people from Europe, Asia and Oceania—appears to be small, the Neanderthals are not extinct, as they live in some of us.

The earliest evidence of modern humans in Australia dates back to roughly 50,000 years ago. Genetic studies suggest a major early human expansion out of Africa, which, in turn, led to the colonization of Australia. It is widely suggested that the early travelers followed the Southern coastline of Asia crossing about 250 kilometers of sea, and reached Australia. According to Wells, the Aborigines of Australia are the descendants of the first wave of migration out of Africa.

According to Spencer Wells, a second wave of Homo sapiens left Africa around 45,000 years ago, multiplied, and then settled in the Middle East. Smaller groups also went to India and China. The remains of one of the earliest modern humans to inhabit East Asia were unearthed in a cave in China in 2007, dating back to 39,000-42,000 years ago. The Asian population became paler over time, isolated by mountains and the sea for many generations, and exposed to a colder climate and less sunlight than in Africa. According to Erlandson, human groups probably followed coastal routes to the Americas and South East Asia after leaving Africa.

Around 40,000 years ago, as the Ice Age ended and temperatures became warmer, humans moved into Central Asia. They found grassy land and multiplied quickly. The journey continued and around 35,000 years ago, small groups left Central Asia for Europe. By 20,000 years ago, the offspring of these ancestors had thus spread into Europe from Central Asia through Russia rather than through the Middle East. They were cut off from others during the ice age. They developed different features in order to adapt to the cold environment, such as light skin to enable sunlight to penetrate through it to synthesize vitamin D.

A recent archaeological find in Russia has shed further light on the migration of modern humans into Europe. Artifacts uncovered at the Kostenki site, south of Moscow, suggest that modern humans were at this spot as early as 45,000 years ago. According to Hoffecker, the first modern humans may have entered Europe through a different route than previously thought. One possible route, some researchers believe, is from Western Asia via the Caucasus Mountains, which lie between the Caspian and Black Seas. He adds that modern humans might have migrated into Central Asia, but then turned back to move into Europe.

From there, around 20,000 years ago, another small group of Central Asians (known today as Eastern Russia's Chukchi) moved farther north, into Siberia and the Arctic Circle. To minimize physical exposure to the extreme cold they developed, over many generations, stubby fingers and short arms and legs. Finally, around 15,000 years ago, another Ice Age ended. Surprisingly enough, a few Arctic families followed the reindeer herds over the Bering Strait land bridge to reach the North American Continent, displaying unbelievable endurance and persistence.

According to the genetic data analyzed by Wells, the initial group who moved south may have included as few as two or twenty people in total. Navaho Indians' DNA matches these early humans, showing that the Native Americans descended from these few families. Their offspring spread out into South America. The Native American acquired distinct physical characteristics because of isolation.

Archaeologists dig worldwide to discover the history and journey of man, who existed too early to leave a written history. Based on such studies, the archaeologists came up with a multi-regional model for man's journey. According to this model, an archaic form of humans left Africa between one and two million years ago, and modern humans evolved from them independently and simultaneously in pockets of Africa, Europe, and Asia.

Supported by Spencer Well's work on studies of the DNA Y chromosome, another model, known as the 'Out of Africa Model', has emerged. According to this model, all modern humans evolved in Africa. They stayed in Africa as humans for generations, and then left in several waves of migration, ultimately replacing any earlier species on this planet. All of the important genetic variations that humans possess today were within humans at that time.

DNA analysis enables us to track our footsteps all the way back to our ancestors. Cell and DNA analysis and development will be reviewed in the next chapter. It is, however, sufficient to note at this point that a human DNA contains all of the intricate codes that make up a human body. It has 23 chromosome pairs with an X-Y chromosome in male and X-X chromosome in female. Each parent contributes half of a child's DNA—the father with the Y chromosome and the mother with the X chromosome. They join to form a new genetic combination. However, DNA in the cells from mitochondria, and the DNA in the male Y chromosome do not recombine or shuffle in the way that ordinary chromosomes or other parts of the genome do.

Thus, they are very stable from one generation to the next. The Y chromosome passes on as a part of DNA from father to son, essentially unchanged through generations except for random mutations. These random mutations can happen naturally and can accumulate. Geneticists call these markers. Once geneticists identify a marker, they can go back in time and trace it to the point at which it first occurred. That would be the most recent common ancestor. They can also use the markers to see how closely humans from different regions of the world are related. Based on this analysis, Gary Stix presented a fascinating description of the traces of a distant past in the July 2008 issue of Scientific American, including the ancient path of migration by tracking genetic markers in the Y Chromosomes of men from different parts of the world.

The DNA evidence concerning our journey points to some remarkable results. A man is still living in Central Asia today whose DNA Y chromosome matches his ancestor's, 2,000 generations or about 40,000 years ago. That ancestor's Y chromosome is responsible for most of mankind all over the world; namely, in Central Asia, India, Europe, Russia, Tundra, Alaska, North and South American continents.

According to Stringer, the fact that one man apparently gave rise to the Y chromosome genes of all moderns does not mean he was our only male ancestor. He goes on to add that what it means is that his male progeny were more prolific breeders or luckier and his Y genes survived while those of his contemporaries did not. Those contemporaries could have passed on many other genes to present-day peoples. Wells agrees with him, adding that the real significance of the date of our common Y-chromosome ancestor is that it effectively gives us an upper limit on when our species began to leave Africa.

As stated, there is another chunk of DNA, which passes through generations relatively unchanged. It is found in a part of the cell called the mitochondria and is transferred from mother to daughter. The most recent male common ancestor identified through the Y chromosome lived 60,000 years ago. However, the most recent female common ancestor traced through mitochondrial DNA lived around 200,000 years ago. Cann and Wilson from the University of California, Berkeley reported that all humans from different populations descended from this single female in Africa.

It is open to debate whether one can identify a single individual as our single common ancestor. Tishkoff says that there is almost certainly not an Adam or Eve. According to him, each of our genes has their own history, which could pass on from different ancestors. It is more likely that a lineage can be traced back to a population of fifty, hundred, or even several thousand people. In 1967, two Homo sapiens skulls dating back 195,000 years were unearthed in Ethiopia, which suggest that the modern humans and their older precursors existed side by side. In 1974, Lucy, a complete hominid skeleton, about 3.5 million years old, was unearthed, which is an important landmark in the search for the origins of humanity.

Another skull discovered in 2006, estimated to be 200,000 to 500,000 years old provides a link between the earlier Homo erectus and the later Homo sapiens. As reported in the journal Science in 2009, a 4.4 million year old animal, Ardipithicus ramidus, was found in Ethiopia in 1992. This might be not be a direct line to humans, but it offers new insights into how we evolved from the common ancestor we share with chimps.

Recently, using different techniques, two teams of scientists separately sequenced large chunks of DNA extracted from the femur of a 38,000-year-old Neanderthal specimen, found 26 years ago in a cave in Croatia. One team sequenced more than 1 million base pairs of the 3.3-billion-pair genome, and the other analyzed 65,000 pairs.

The present-day population in Africa carries a signature of the ancient split in their DNA. However, today's Africans are part of a single population. In 2008, the researchers compiled a 'family tree' of different mitochondrial DNA groupings found in Africa. They believe that a major split occurred near the root of the tree as early as 150,000 years ago. On one side are the mitochondrial lineages, now found predominantly in East and West Africa, and all the maternal lineages found outside Africa. On the other side, there are lineages predominantly found in the Khoi and San (Khoisan); the hunter-gatherer people of Southern Africa. Many African populations today are a mixture of both.

Spencer Wells in his book The Journey of Man: A Genetic Odyssey by Princeton University Press traces human evolution back to our very first ancestor. Wells' work draws on genetics, paleo-anthropology, aloe-climatology, archaeology, psychology, and linguistics. Using the cutting-edge scientific developments of population genetics, he creates a family tree for the whole of humanity. He sums up all the available evidence from the fossil record and explains the effects of the new techniques in genetics. Evidence from excavations presents an interesting picture about our journey.

Scientists do not agree on various events described during our journey. For example, in February 2006, at the annual meeting of the American Association for the Advancement of Science, they outlined a new thinking about migration to North America. According to this thinking, the first humans to spread across North America might have been seal hunters from France and Spain. This runs counter to the long-held belief described above that the first human entry into the Americas was a crossing of a land-ice bridge that spanned the Bering Strait about 13,500 years ago.

New thinking based on recent studies indicates that the glaciers bridging Siberia and Alaska began receding around 17,000 to 13,000 years ago. This left very little chance for people to walk from one continent to the other. Furthermore, archaeologist Dennis Stanford of the Smithsonian Institution sees a divergence of many characteristics when he places American spearheads, called Clovis points, side-by-side with Siberian points.

Instead, Stanford believes that Clovis points are a closer match to Solutrean style tools, dating from approximately 19,000 years ago. It suggests that the American people who made Clovis points also made Solutrean points before that. This hypothesis presents a problem. Solutrean toolmakers lived in France and Spain, and scientists know of no land-ice bridge that spanned that entire gap. They may have even made their way into the floating ice chunks that unite immense harp seal populations in Canada and Europe each year.

According to a recent study, reported in Nature magazine, our evolutionary cousin, the Neanderthal may have survived in Europe much longer than previously thought. It suggests that the Neanderthal species may have lived in Gorham's Cave on Gibraltar up to 24,000 years ago; dying out about 35,000 years ago at a time when modern humans were advancing across the continent. Recently, Geneticist Svante Paabo and his team claim to have isolated the long segments of genetic material from a 45,000-year-old Neanderthal fossil from Croatia. Their work should reveal how closely related the Neanderthal species was to modern humans, Homo sapiens.

Admittedly, there are gaps in the history and journey of humankind. There are also disagreements. Nevertheless, there is a lot more agreement in this field today than there was a decade ago. It is obvious that more and more insight will come from closer collaboration between various disciplines. Stringer says that greater discussion and collaboration between geneticists and paleoanthropologists would be good for both. According to him, the studies of recent DNA are the studies of the genes of the survivors. Such studies cannot tell us anything about non-survivors, such as the Neanderthals and the Solo man in Java. We still require fossils, archaeology, and ancient DNA for the whole picture of human evolution.

Despite some disagreement, we can look back at our common origin, history, and journey with new respect. It has been a long and strange journey with increasing realization that our species has one shared history. It is also interesting to note that our journey has picked up pace during the past couple of centuries. The 'cultural evolution' discussed later, is based on information processed by the brain rather than slow genetic changes. It is responsible for this faster pace.

Today, the protein sequences in our genome are genetically 99.9 % identical to others. In other words, only one-tenth of 1% or one base pair per thousand base pairs is different, which still amounts to about 3 million base pairs out of billion pairs in human DNA. This difference might account for changes such as, skin color, body shape, eye and hair color and shape. These superficial differences are due to very few gene mutations that came about due to infections or adjustment to different climatic conditions. Essentially, we are all the same genetically except for these superficial differences. These small differences also appear across the board. Therefore, in one sense, we are all same, and in another sense, we are all different due to the 0.1% superficial differences in our protein sequences. However, we must remember that the DNA of each individual has distinct features, which identify that person.

1.3   Life before Humans

Let us now briefly visit the period before humans appeared on this planet. DNA analysis has enabled us to track our footsteps all the way back to chimpanzees. According to DNA and other evidence from excavations, an interesting picture emerges about our evolution from primitive life. It is difficult to pinpoint the origin of humanity.

The recent discovery of a 4.2 million year old fossil in North East Ethiopia in 2006 helped scientists to fill in the gaps. It shows how human ancestors made the giant leap from one species to another. This discovery is important according to Ethiopian anthropologist Berhane Asfaw. The newest fossil, the species Australopithecus anamensis, was found in the region, where seven other human-like species spanning nearly 6 million years and three major phases of human development were previously discovered. Asfaw thinks that we just found the chain of evolution, the continuity through time. The scientific journal Nature reported these findings in April 2006.

An article by Kate Wong in the January 2003 Scientific American states that a complete cranium unearthed in Northern Chad's Djurab Desert dates back to nearly 7 million years ago. According to Brunet, this may be the point in history where our lineage diverged from the chimpanzee. However, a husband and wife team, Moya-Sola and Kohler, recently unearthed a 13-million-year-old ape from the new ape species in Spain—Pierolapithecus catalaunicus. It has a body of an ape, with fingers like chimp and the upright posture of humans.

According to an article in Science magazine in November 2006, the 13-million-year old ape is perhaps the last common ancestor to all the living humans and great apes. Professor Howell at the University of Berkeley finds it a remarkable find. The group of great apes still in existence includes humans, chimps, gorillas, and orangutans. The group is thought to have split from the lesser apes, such as gibbons and siamangs around 14—16 million years ago. According to Moya-Sola, the newly discovered species probably also lived in Africa, however fossil records in Africa for that period are scarce and rare.

In 2006, Soojin Yi and colleagues at the Georgia Institute of Technology said that they found genetic evidence that might more closely relate chimpanzees to humans, than to gorillas and orangutans. Experts have long known that humans and chimpanzees share similar DNA, and are in fact 96%identical on the genetic level. Most experts agree that humans split from a common ancestor with chimpanzees several million years ago and that gorillas and orangutans separated much earlier. However, it is difficult to date precisely when, although most recent studies have put the date at about 5—7 million years ago.

A new controversial study claims that chimpanzees and humans split from a common ancestor just 4 million years ago—a much shorter time than current estimates of 5—7 million years ago. According to Dr. Asger Hobolth of North Carolina State University, the primate evolution is a central topic in biology, and one can obtain much information from DNA sequence data. The basis of the theory of a molecular clock, used to track evolution, is the premise that all DNA mutates at a certain rate. It is not always a steady rate, but it evens out over the millennia.

They used a well-known type of calculation not previously applied to genetics to come up with their own 'molecular clock' estimate of when humans became uniquely human. In this study, the researchers compared the DNA of chimpanzees, humans and our next-closest ancestor, the gorilla, as well as orangutans. The study, published in the Public Library of Science journal PLoS Genetics, states that assuming orangutan divergence occurred 18 million years ago, speciation time of human and chimpanzee is consistently around 4 million years ago.

Stepping back further in time, archaeologists paint a fascinating picture of evolution from the fossils records dating back about 400 million years ago. Around 360 million years ago, some species of fish

13

even tinkered with evolution tools and evolved into tetra pods that came out of water and walked on land. Species of creatures walking on land, such as dinosaurs, go through several transitions, such as their sudden disappearance about 65 million years ago and the subsequent evolution of a different species of mammals. Our ancestors appeared on the planet around 2.5 million years ago. Recent evidence unearthed in Mongolia indicates that the mammal species first appeared as the dinosaurs made their exit from our plant 65 million years ago.

Stepping back even farther beyond 400 million years, we discover fossils of bacteria from 3.5 billion years ago, which is responsible for the origin of all subsequent life forms. However, this may not be the very first form of life since such complex bacterium has to evolve from somewhere. According to Goodenough, some organisms must have preceded the bacteria fossil record. We may never know the common ancestor for all of the creatures on this planet. Science is unlikely to trace all the steps actually followed in the creation of life. Life, since its creation, has evolved and erased most of the footprints along the way. Fig. 1.2, illustrates the various interesting steps in the journey from the Big Bang to the appearance of our human ancestor.

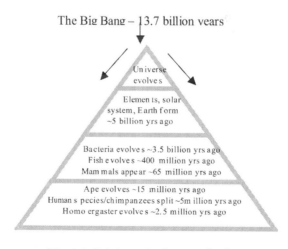

Fig. 1.2 Origin & Evolution of Life

Chapter 2
Science & Mysteries of Life

2.1   *Introduction*

During this phase of our journey, we discover what science has to say about the origin and evolution of life (Fig. 2.1).

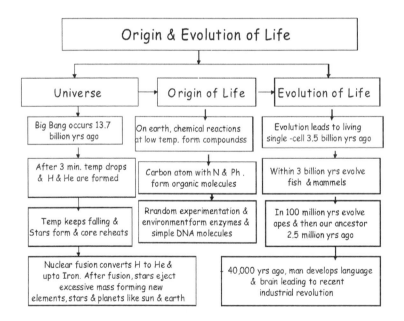

Fig. 2.1—Origin & Evolution of Life

We visit Darwin's theory of the evolution of life, before examining life at the cellular level and the miracle of life originating from a cell's DNA. A series of questions are raised that science must answer, including: "Can science provide answer to the question, what is life?" "With its current limitations, can it help us understand the meaning and purpose of life?" Finally, within this chapter, we visit religion to see what it has to offer concerning the origin and meaning of life.

2.2   Scientific Meaning of Life

"What is life and how did it begin?" Science first answers this question by explaining the origin and evolution of the universe. The Big Bang created the universe. Space expanded and as it cooled down from billions of degrees, nuclei and atoms of lighter elements such as hydrogen form. These elements constitute over 95% of the ordinary matter in the universe even today. Due to gravity, the gases pull together forming stars and galaxies. Depending on the amount of gas in stars, gravitational force keeps squeezing the gas molecules and shrinking its size.

The gravitational squeeze heats up the core of the star. As gas molecules strike each other, it provides the temperature and the environment to form the remaining elements of ordinary matter. Depending on its size, a star has different fates. For example, it can become a black hole or explode spewing out all the elements in space. If a star explodes, the matter spewed out comes together again due to gravity, forming planets, etc. Earth is one such planet. Organic compounds form as various atoms and molecules react chemically with Carbon.

Such a sequence of events eventually leads to the formation of enzymes, proteins, and different cells, which lead to the constitution of different forms of animate objects. Human DNA is one such entity, which evolves and leads to human beings; constructed from the map in the human's cell DNA. DNA molecules for all living objects are essentially composed of the same four basic pairs repeated in a certain sequence. This will be discussed further in this chapter.

We distinguish living or animate objects from non-living or inanimate objects in a simple manner. A living entity must essentially have all the following characteristics:

1.   Capability to sustain itself
2.   Capability to reproduce itself
3.   Capability to propagate

The human brain distinguishes us from other animals and living entities and thus, we consider human life superior because of our advanced brain. It gives us the ability to think intelligently; to process data and optimize our course of action based on past stored data and values, or stored learning patterns. The brain gives every individual a distinct personality based on its efficiency to perform various functions, and the acquired/stored 'values' that decide one's optimal criteria for action.

Our brain projects our personality not just for the outside world; it also gives meaning to the word, 'I'. It takes all the critical decisions, projects our personality, and gives meaning to life. A human brain cannot only think "intelligently" it has also evolved to a state where it can integrate and perform the following functions more efficiently.

1.   Coordinate visual, audio, smell, taste, and touch data received from multiple sensors.
2.   Process the data to extract information.
3.   Compare the extracted information with stored information and update storage.
4.   Decide the optimum course of action based on criteria reflecting our 'values'.
5.   Transmit signals to various organs of the body to implement the course of action.
6.   Monitor, adapt, and control the action process to achieve the intended results.

These areas will be discussed in-depth in the final chapter. The brain system, the most important master controller,is essentially composed of neuron cells. The brain optimizes our decisions using various optimality criteria and our 'values'; which are coded, modified, and reinforced by the way we live our life, dictate the optimality criteria. All the emotions, feelings, and actions originate in the brain due to interaction with the outside world through the body sensors.

To sum up, science essentially defines life or a living entity as a sophisticated mechanism put together by DNA. This DNA stores all information about life's mechanism in a coded form. It exercises a strict control at every stage to keep the mechanism functioning according to the code. Different types of cells, formed from the same DNA due to the activation of different genes, go on to form various subsystems. These subsystems include the nervous system for information transmission and the digestive system for providing nourishment to the body's cells for sustenance, etc. These subsystems have their own feedback controls to insure smooth functioning. The internal feedback systems also control various organs, such as lungs for air in-take and outlet, the heart and other muscles.

Science does not support the notion of soul. It states that the so-called conscience or awareness is the result of the projection of a person's individuality by the mind. Science also attributes the evolution of life to chance interactions, chemical reactions, mutations, and principle of natural selection enunciated by Darwin. Before we proceed to discuss in-depth what modern science has revealed about living cells and life, let us step back in history to visit Darwin and analyze his theories about the evolution of life.

2.3   Darwin's Evolution

Darwin proposed the Theory of Evolution—a set of principles that attempt to explain how life appeared on earth in all its various forms. It is the only scientific theory that explains the diversity of life on Earth. Are all the different species we see today formed as predicted by Darwin's theory? The Theory of Evolution can explain why bacteria and mosquitoes become resistant to antibiotics and insecticides. It can also successfully predict, for example, that X-ray exposure would lead to thousands of mutations in fruit flies. The theory can also explain microevolution; e.g., the evolution of bacteria, etc.

However, there is a great deal of controversy regarding its application to macroevolution; e.g., the evolution of man from small organisms. Many people, mostly religious-minded, have serious reservations about the Theory of Evolution. They point to several problems with Darwin's theory and suggest faith-based theories such as the Theory of Creation and Intelligent Design instead. This opposing theory asserts that one can better explain several features of living beings as the work of the 'Designer', rather than the random process or natural selection proposed by Darwin's Theory of Evolution.

A theory is usually repeatedly tested and widely accepted if it can make verifiable predictions about a natural phenomenon. Obviously, the Theory of Evolution cannot completely answer several questions at this point. Darwin proposed the Theory of Evolution in 1850 when we knew so little about cell chemistry and DNA, etc. It may need to be modified as we learn even more about the effect of mutations on DNA and about living cells. It is common in science to modify a theory. People create new theories and modify existing ones to explain the unexplained. For example, Einstein modified Newton's theory of gravitation to answer some nagging questions. Currently the Theory of Evolution can be described in simple terms. Suppose we have a set of living organisms with certain random characteristics

1. It can reproduce.
2. Its offspring can inherit traits.
3. It has variability of traits.

In other words, the set of objects has the same random characteristics described in Darwin's Theory of Evolution. Suppose one suddenly puts such a set of organisms in a restrictive environment that is different from the current environment. Random changes and gene mutations start and continue, changing the organisms. The organisms that can best adapt to the changing environment survive. If changes in the environment are minor and there are no supply constraints, then all members of the surviving set can resist the change and survive. Severe changes and/or limited supplies force them to compete for the limited supplies, and only those that survive can adapt to environmental imbalances and have the necessary traits better suited for survival. The surviving members reproduce and pass on these traits to the offspring with some variability.

The offspring continue to adjust and adapt, using all possible options such as gene mutations and competing with each other for mating selection. Nature or the restrictive environment selects or allows the survival of only those that can withstand continuous changes and adapt. Others simply perish. The surviving offspring, more adaptive to the environment, keep on improving and pass on these survival traits with certain variability to their offspring. It is, of course, possible that environmental changes may become extreme for a species and the entire set might perish. The disappearance of dinosaurs is a classic example.

The variation in the expression of traits occurs in all plants and animals. This is the reason that individuals in a population are rarely identical. Genes control the expression of traits. Furthermore, genes during meiosis do not always perfectly replicate and the offspring of an organism respond to the environment differently. Mutations and the recombination of genes by the offspring's two parents and infections provide certain changes. Such changes can decide if it will survive and pass on its characteristics to its progeny.

Darwin wrote in his book, The Origin of Species:

> "Natural selection acts solely by accumulating slight, successive, favorable variations, it can produce no great or sudden modification; it can act only by very short and slow steps. Natural selection also acts by competition."

He said that it is neither the strongest of the species that survives, nor the most intelligent, but the one most responsive to change.

> "If it could be demonstrated that any complex organ existed which could not possibly have been formed by numerous, successive, slight modifications, my theory would absolutely break down."
> -Charles Darwin, *The Origin of Species* (1859).

Natural Selection and Universal Principle of Change

The type of natural selection and incremental changes at the genetic level, described above, is in fact at the heart of Darwin's Principle of Natural Selection for evolution. We can sum up The Principle of Natural Selection in the 'if-then' form. For example, *If:*

- the organisms reproduce, and
- the offspring inherit traits from their progenitor(s), and
- there is variability of traits, and
- the changing environment cannot support all members of a growing population.

Then:

- members of the population with less-adaptive traits (determined by the environment) will die out, and
- members with more-adaptive traits (determined by environment) will thrive.

The result is the evolution of species.

As previously stated, the natural selection process removes the individuals with traits that cannot adapt to a particular environment. It thus increases the frequency of 'fit' individuals in a population. Individuals that survive and reproduce perpetuate the species by passing on the genes conferring 'fitness' to the next generation. Thus, natural selection leads to adaptation. Such a process leads to the evolution of all forms of life that we see around us.

The experiments in a laboratory confirm that one can control the frequency of a trait occurring in subsequent generations by artificially selecting for, or against, a specific trait. During evolution, the evolving ability to make decisions gives living entities the choice for selecting the course for survival in the changing environment.

Note that the underlying theme is always the continuous search by objects or species for a stable equilibrium state in the presence of environmental changes or imbalance, and the given constraints. The state of equilibrium achieved is a function of the following elements.

1. The current state of equilibrium

2.   The object characteristics (which might be non-deterministic with multiple choices),

3.   The magnitude of the environmental change, energy imbalance, available choices, or traits.

This is simply a restatement of the Universal Principle of Change (UPC) introduced in my second book—*Knowing the Unknown—II Mysteries of The Universe—Past, Present, and Future*—which includes these three elements in defining the process of change, as follows.

> *"Change takes place in a region of space only when two or more force fields interact with each other, disturbing the present state of equilibrium for matter or field(s). The state of matter or field(s) in the affected region continues to change, following the path of The Least Action and maintaining the energy balance through energy exchange and/or transformation. A stable state of equilibrium is reached only when there is no more transient variation of the interacting force fields with time. The state of equilibrium achieved is a function of the three elements, current state, object characteristics, and the environment"*
> *- Manohar Lal*

- Darwin's Journey to Genetic Evolution

It is interesting to trace Darwin's path to genetic evolution and the Natural Selection principle. Let us first narrate the interesting events that led Darwin to come up with the Principle of Natural Selection and the Theory of Evolution. Darwin, a twenty-two year old man graduating from Cambridge University with a degree in Theology, sailed as a naturalist on the British Navy's H.M.S. Beagle mapping expedition (1831-1836). Darwin's observations on this voyage led him to the Theory of Evolution. He wrote extensive notes on his observations during this journey and about his ideas about the evolution (Fig.2.2)

Fig. 2.2—Darwin and His Notes

His visit to the Galápagos Islands in the eastern Pacific Ocean was particularly important to him for understanding what causes plants and animals to evolve. Darwin identified 13 species of finches in the Galápagos Islands, each with different beak shapes (Fig. 2.3).

Fig. 2.3—Beak Varieties of Finches on the Galápagos Islands

He was puzzled since he knew of only one species of this bird on the mainland of South America, 600 miles to the east, where the finches had presumably originated. He also observed that the beak varieties were associated with diets, based on different foods.

He thought that the original South American finches, on reaching the islands, dispersed to different environments where they had to adapt to different conditions. Over many generations, there was a change in their anatomy, which allowed them to get enough food to survive and reproduce. One could easily conclude, as Lamarck did, that the environment alone altered the shape of individuals and that these acquired changes were then inherited.

A species can be split into subsets due to several reasons. For example, a mountain range or an ocean can cause such a split. These subsets evolve into distinct species as they pick up different mutations and create different gene pools. Darwin did not believe that the environment alone was responsible for the changes within the finch populations. He thought that the variability of traits already existed. The nature or the environment just selected the most suitable beak shape over less useful ones, by letting the fittest survive. Darwin called this the Principle of Natural Selection, and his supporters described this process as the 'survival of the fittest'.

Up until now, we have discovered 1.8 million known plant and animal species, which are being assembled in the Encyclopedia of Life, a $100m project that aims to detail all species in a net archive. It will have individual species pages that include photographs, video, audio, and maps collected and written by experts. This archive, to be built over 10 years, could help conservation efforts as well as being a useful tool for education. According to the Executive Director of the project, Dr Edwards, The Encyclopedia of Life would provide valuable biodiversity and conservation information to anyone, anywhere, at any time. The first 30,000 pages of this vast encyclopedia were unveiled in 2008.

2.4 *Evolution Vs Creation*

To summarize, there is plenty of present and past evidence for some sort of evolutionary process. We see it in bacteria and insects today, and we see it in fossil records through the development of millions of species over millions of years. The fossil record indicates that hundreds of millions of new species were created over hundreds of millions of years. However, as stated earlier, many people especially creationists have serious reservations about Darwin's Theory of Evolution.

The creationists believe that God intervened to create human beings. God and His role in creation will be discussed in detail the next chapter. However, the primary argument for the theory of creation or Intelligent Design is that evolution and natural selection alone could not lead, over billions of years, to the type of complexity observed in the human body. They claim that natural selection is capable of achieving only trivial variations within a fundamentally stable species. Furthermore, the fossil record has long been a problem for Darwinists, according to the creationists. This record does not shown the steady, gradual, progressive changes that Darwin's theory predicts and requires.

Proponents of the theory of creation or Intelligent Design ask you to look at the set of features, at the complexity, and look at how they work together. They claim that it is inconceivable that they came about by chance mutations or evolution by gradual change. There is a flood of recent books challenging evolution. For example in the book, What Darwin Didn't Know by Geoffrey Simmons and William Dembski, the authors state that human body is indeed complex and involves vast amounts of design. They try to make the case for Intelligent Design and creation rather than evolution.

Everyone agrees that the human body is complex, but scientists say that it does not necessarily imply that the working systems of the human body were 'pre-planned' and designed to work together right from the start. This debate will be reviewed in-depth during further chapters of this book. Let us continue our journey and visit life at a cellular level, attempting to understand the miracle of life originating from a cell's DNA.

2.5   *Modern Genetics*

During the mid 1800s, when Darwin advanced the Theory of Evolution, he knew very little about cell biology. It was simply because very little was known about cells at that time. We thought of cells as simple globs of protoplasm, which were mere building blocks of a body like bricks for building a house. Now, modern science and research in genetics tell us that cells are the most complex machines in the universe that can live on their own in the right environment. We must focus on progress made in the field of genetics to understand human cells.

Visiting the field of genetics is important, because genetic coding holds the key to life. The evolution of species is essentially the modification of its DNA molecule, and genetics is mostly about the DNA molecule. Furthermore, it relates closely to chemistry and several other areas of science. It directs lifeless organic chemical compounds to assemble in a complex manner according to the code; eventually leading to the creation of life by assembling cells that can multiply, mutate, and adapt or change.

We start our journey by visiting the remarkable progress made in the field of genetics during the last century. It started with Mendel in 1900, who teased the laws of heredity from the pea plants. By the mid 1900s, scientists had unlocked the molecular secrets of heredity. They showed that long, winding stretches of DNA genetics encoded the information, with each cell copying this information before dividing and multiplying itself.

The end of the twentieth century witnessed the completion of human genome sequencing in terms of the four base elements: A, C, T, and G. The Human Genome Project (HGP) successfully sequenced these three billion base pairs before the end of the 1900s. The human genome sequence consists of three billion letters of genetic instructions that make up a human being, compared to three million base pairs for bacteria in yogurt, for example. The sequence of base pairs is similar to a string of binary number code used to characterize information.

In other words, a genome contains the master blueprint for all cellular structures and all the activities of the cells and organisms. In the nucleus of each cell, we find human genome that consists of the longest molecule—called DNA—tightly coiled threads of deoxyribonucleic acid and associated protein molecules, organized into structures called chromosomes.

The human body contains trillions of cells. Fig. 2.4 below shows a cell, chromosomes, and DNA. The encoded DNA molecule in each cell, comprised of different chemicals, is responsible for human life. It makes the DNA encoded information accessible. It interprets and executes this information to make proteins. It also decides our appearance and the way we feel.

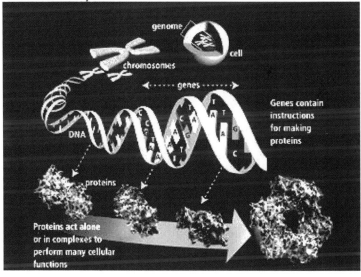

Fig. 2.4—Cell, Chromosomes and DNA
(Source: U.S. Department of Energy)

Let us discuss various elements that hold the key to life one-by-one.

- **Human Cells**

1.   There are 50 trillion to 100 trillion cells in a human body.

2.   They belong to a family of over 200 different kinds of cells.

3.   Each cell is made up of exchangeable basic element atoms and molecules. For example, oxygen and carbon dioxide molecules are exchanged in lungs in a thousandth of a second. The sodium and potassium ions in brain cells exchange about three hundred times per second.

4.   All cells are genetically identical, controlled by the same DNA molecule inside the nucleus of a cell. The DNA molecule does not change much and it has remained distinctly humanlike for several million years, evolving genetically over billions of years.

5.   At conception, a DNA molecule inside the nucleus of a cell is fused together from two sets of chromosomes; one set given by each parent.

6.   On day one, it starts with a fertilized egg. The developing embryo—called blastocyst, which consists of an outer cell mass, and eventually becomes the fetus in the womb of a pregnant woman, multiplies into 100 to 150 cells within a week.

7.   These Embryonic Stem (ES) cells continue to multiply and begin to specialize and differentiate themselves. The embryo—called a gastrula at this stage—contains three distinctive germ layers. The descendants of these three layers go on to form hundreds of different tissue types in the human body. In addition to the embryonic stem (ES) cells, the adult stem cells are also found in the bone marrow. The best known such stem cell—called hematopoietic stem cell—gives rise mostly to blood and immune cells.

8. The same DNA molecule creates all kinds of specialized cells (the brain, heart, skin, liver, etc.) each with different functions and life spans, by activating different genes in the same DNA molecule. Each cell functions differently, not because its DNA is different but because different cells activate different genes in the same DNA.

9. The body continually reproduces new cells and replaces the old cells as they die. Each cell has an allotted life span. The heart can apparently last a lifetime without reproducing. Contrary to earlier beliefs, the body can make new brain cells (neurons) and connections. Other cells reproduce and replace the old cells as they die. For example, a typical cell in a liver replaces itself after a life span of several years. A typical red blood cell is replaced after its life span of about 2-3 months, and an olfactory cell in the nose is replaced after about four weeks.

10. According to US scientists, just one brain cell is capable of holding short-term memories vital for our everyday life. Scientists have compared the differences between the brain's long-term and short-term memory, likening them to the RAM of a computer compared to its hard drive.

So many cells in our body often die and the material within it changes, but our body outlasts these changes. We do not have the same body cells we were born with. Various cells are replaced regularly. However, our DNA molecule—the essential element of each cell—shown in Fig. 2.4, does not change much. It has remained humanlike for several million years, evolving genetically over billions of years.

- DNA

1. A DNA molecule consists of two strands that wrap around each other, resembling a twisted ladder, as shown in Fig. 2.4.

2.   The strands of DNA, if unwound and tied together, would stretch more than 5 feet, but its width would only be 50 trillionth of an inch.

3.   This slender long thread for each organism encodes all the information necessary for building and maintaining life.

4.   Each strand of the DNA molecule is a linear arrangement of repetitive similar units called nucleotides.

5.   Each nucleotide is composed of one sugar, one phosphate and a nitrogenous chemical called base.

6.   DNA has four different types of bases: A, C, T, and G

7.   (A—Adenine, C—Cystocine, T—Thymine, and G—Guanine), as shown in Fig. 2.5.

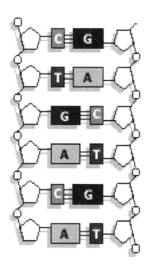

Fig. 2.5—Base Pairs forming the 'Code of Life

9.   Adenine (A) bonds with Thymine (T); Cytosine (C) bonds with Guanine (G)

10. These base pairs form the 'code of life'. There are about 2.9 billion base pairs in the human genome, which are wound into 24 distinct bundles, or chromosomes.

- Chromosomes

1. Human genome or a complete set of DNA contains about 3 billion base pairs.

2. The 3 billion base pairs in a set of DNA are organized into physically separate microscopic units called chromosomes, which are visible under a light microscope.

3. DNA in the human genome is arranged into 24 distinct chromosomes.

4. Chromosomes contain about equal parts of DNA and proteins. Each chromosomal DNA part contains approximately 50-250 million base pairs.

5. The nucleus of each human cell contains two sets of chromosomes; one set provided by each parent. Each set has 22 autosomes and X and/or Y sex chromosomes (a female has XX and a male has XY chromosomes).

- Genes

1. Genes are specific sequences of bases that encode instructions on how to make proteins.

2. All genes are arranged linearly along the chromosomes. Human genes are essentially protein coding sequences, often separated by extensive non-protein coding sequences on a DNA molecule.

3. Genes comprise around 2% of the human genome, with the remaining 98% consisting of non-coding regions.

4. There are 20-40,000 genes coded with base pairs in the DNA, which are used by human cells to make proteins. Protein molecules build and maintain our bodies.

5. Genes get more attention since they are responsible for protein production and they are believed to be responsible for almost everything that happens inside our body.

6. Genes make over half a million human proteins in our body—the enzymes that digest our food, the hormones

that control our reproduction, and the brain chemicals that govern our moods, thoughts, and personalities.

7. Each chromosome contains many genes, which are the basic physical and functional units of heredity. A tiny change in a single gene can have very large effect on a species.

8. Genes, identically present in each of our cells, act in different combinations. They turn on and off like switches several times a second and send complex signals through chemical reactions to our cells, directing their activity.

- Proteins

1. Proteins, manufactured according to the encoded instructions from the genes, are large complex molecules made up of a long chain of chemicals called amino acids.

2. Proteins perform most life functions and even make up the majority of cellular structures.

3. Proteins direct most of the activities we associate with life; directing cells to grow, communicate, reproduce, and even die.

4. A cell produces abnormal proteins when a gene mutates and one or more base pairs change in sequence. This can cause diseases including cancer—a disease of the cells. Studying such mutations is the key to developing various drugs and treatment for different types of cancers.

5. A DNA molecule is the same in each cell. The difference between various types of cells (e.g. between brain cells and bone cells) in a human body is that different genes are active in their DNA molecules, enabling cells to produce different kinds of proteins.

6. When a gene is activated, each specific sequence of three DNA bases (e.g. GCA) called codons, directs the cell's protein-making machinery to add a specific amino acid (e.g. amino acid alanine) to the protein.

7.   The resulting amino acid chains thus form and each chain twists and folds into an intricate three-dimensional shape making a specific protein.

8.   There are only 20 different amino acids formed by various codons. A protein coded by an average sized gene (3,000 base pairs) will contain a chain of approximately 1,000 amino acids from these 20 basic amino acids.

- Information in the Genome

Scientists are working to decipher the massive amount of information contained in the letters of our genome. They are attempting to translate seemingly endless strings of As, Cs, Ts, and Gs. As stated previously, about 30,000 genes, protein-coding sequences, make up less than 2% of the DNA molecule in a human chromosome. The rest of the base pair sequencing (over 98%), including the introns within the genes and the long stretches of intergenic DNA between genes, were assumed to be evolutionary junk until recently. Geneticists dismissed it as 'junk'.

However, geneticists are now focusing on this 'junk'. They believe that its functions may include providing chromosomal structural integrity regulating where, when, and in what quantity proteins are made. Geneticists have recently discovered that this part of the genome influences the development and distinctive traits of all organisms, including humans. An interesting article in the November 2005 issue of *Scientific American* throws further light on this.

As revealed by a close-up view of the human genome, its innermost workings appear to be far more complex than first thought. The journals *Nature and Genome Research* published the results of this study, carried out on just 1% of our DNA code. It challenges the view that genes are the main players in driving our biochemistry. Instead, the study suggests that the 'junk' DNA and other elements weave together an intricate control network.

In material science, we have a periodic table of elements for matter. One can explain different compounds and forms arising from these elements and the way they interact. In a similar manner in life sciences, a genome is the biological equivalent of the periodic table. Landers said recently that we should be able to explain the behavior of all cells and organisms, in terms of the interaction of the components of this biology's periodic table. This table has all the genes, which make up a human, a mouse, a fly, a tree, or any living entity.

The genome of the black cottonwood (Populus trichocarpa) for example, was sequenced in 2006 as part of a four-year international project led by US institutions. The work, reported in *Science* journal in 2006, shows that the poplar tree has far less DNA in its cells than humans or other mammals, but twice the number of genes. Researchers believe that this new information will lead to a better understanding of plant biology and evolution. Scientists are already enumerating the genome sequence of many other organisms.

We have the complete code of several living organisms, insects and animals, viruses, bacteria, yeast, etc. According to an agreement to be signed at the third International Barcode of Life conference in Mexico City in 2009, hundreds of experts from 50 nations agreed on a "DNA barcode" system that gives every plant on Earth a unique genetic fingerprint. Today we also have the complete map of human genome—detailed information about the DNA molecule in a cell.

We now have the key to the greatest library on the planet—a place where evolution has been keeping notes for over 2.5 billion years. Unfortunately, this biological periodic table is too long with tens of thousands of genes. By activating different genes in the same DNA molecule, different types of cells and over half a million different proteins can be made. This makes us what we are.

- Genetic Revolution

The Human Genome Project enabled scientists to identify all the genes that make up humans. The function of most of our genes remains a mystery, despite the massive advances made in sequencing the DNA in the human genome. We need to understand this function in order to identify the genes that play important roles in cancer and other diseases. Recently, scientists launched a major international initiative to achieve several research goals related to the human genome in a systematic manner. The next stage is set to map all 35,000 or so genes and uncover the functions and complex interactions of each. Such an effort is likely to provide vital information about how cancer disrupts the normal functioning of our cells, which could lead to new drug treatments to prevent this from happening.

Geneticists are identifying different genes almost daily that are all responsible for different actions. DNA micro-arrays gene chips are allowing us to study genes, using precision robotics and tiny slides dotted with thousands of DNA samples, which represent different genes. Such an endeavor—dissecting the function of a single gene from around 35,000 genes—has become possible due to the discovery of RNA interference.

RNA interference, first discovered in the obscure nematode worm, plays a crucial role in de-coding information from genes to build new proteins. However, the nematode also uses tiny pieces of RNA to switch off specific rogue genes that would otherwise cause it harm. Genes produce their effect by sending molecules called messenger RNA to the protein-making machinery of a cell. RNA interference destroys this RNA and prevents the production of the specific protein, thus effectively silencing the gene.

Researchers have found that synthetically produced RNA sequences can target genes in human cells. Scientists are using RNA interference to create cells in which all genes are fully functional, bar one, and analyze how the loss of individual genes affects cell function. According to Downward, dismantling cancer at the level of its genes using RNA interference would enable us to find out what we need to remove from a cancerous cell in order to make it normal again.

Frontier technologies are helping these efforts. Bioinformatics technology helps make sense of the information in a genome and Proteomics technology studies proteins. RNA interference technology helps study built-in defensive mechanisms in a human cell, and a high throughput X-ray crystallography helps in the 3-D modeling of proteins.

Two Nobel prizes awarded in 2006 for work in this field bear out the importance of such studies. Fire and Mello received the Nobel Prize in Medicine for discovering a fundamental mechanism for controlling the flow of genetic information, using the RNA Interference Technique. Professor Kornberg from Stanford received the 2006 Nobel Prize in Chemistry for his work on the eukaryotic transcription in cells.

Transcription is an important step in the process by which cells build proteins from DNA. Kornberg's studies on transcription described how one takes information from genes and converts it to the molecules, known as messenger RNA. These molecules shuttle the information to the cells' protein-making machinery. His work is important because disturbances in the transcription process are involved in many human illnesses such as cancer, heart disease and various kinds of inflammation.

Recent work by Bygren and other scientists has also shown that extreme environmental changes can accelerate the evolution process and alter the genetic activity passed onto the next generation. This work has given birth to a new science called epigenetics. In simple terms, epigenetics is the study of changes in gene activity, which do not involve alterations to the genetic code. Instead, such changes are passed down to at least one successive generation.

The cellular material, epigenome, governs these patterns of gene expression. This material sits on top of the genome, just outside it. These epigenetic marks tell several genes to either switch on or off. Therefore, environmental factors such as diet, stress, and prenatal nutrition can make an imprint on genes through epigenetic marks, which are passed from one generation to the next.

2.6   *Does Science have the Answers?*

Does science have all the answers? Obviously, it does not! Science has some answers. Science confirms that a chemical reaction, radiation or an infection can modify a base pair in the DNA strand to create a mutation. Such a modification can lead to the creation of a new protein or enzyme. The Theory of Evolution explains why and how strands of a DNA change. The theory also proposes that billions of such mutations are responsible for all the life forms we see today. It suggests the following chain of events:

1.   An initial self-replicating molecule spontaneously forms.
2.   Self-replicating molecules evolve into single-cell organisms.
3.   Single-cell organisms evolve into multi-cell organisms.
4.   Multi-cell organisms evolve into vertebrates, such as fish, etc.

In the process, DNA structures evolve from the asexual single-strand format found in bacteria today. They evolve into the dual-strand chromosomal format found in all higher life forms. The number of chromosomes increases from 5 for fruit flies to 20 for mice, 23 for humans and 39 for dogs, etc. However, science cannot yet explain how these mutations can create new chromosomes, lengthen a strand of DNA, or grow a genome. For example, selective breeding has not changed the basic genome in various animals. It has not increased the DNA. The breeding process simply selects different genes from the existing gene pool, and creates different breeds.

Another point that the opponents of the Theory of Evolution make, is that we have not seen monkeys turning into humans, or one species turning into other species during our history of thousands of years. According to them, if we left members of a species free to breed for thousands of years, we would still find the same species when we visit them after that period. They are correct but this argument does not go against evolution. Evolutionists have always said that the genetic evolution is not drastic and takes place at an extremely slow pace, and one cannot easily perceive it.

Evolution is indeed an extremely slow process. Darwin himself said in his book.

> *"The chief cause of our natural unwillingness to admit that one species has given birth to other and distinct species is that we are always slow*

in admitting any great change of which we do not see the intermediate
steps...The mind cannot possibly grasp the full meaning of the term
of a hundred million years; it cannot add up and perceive the full ef-
fects of many slight variations, accumulated during an almost infinite
number of generations."
Darwin- *The Origin of Species* (1859)

Carl Sagan also writes the following in *The Dragons of Eden* that the time scale for evolutionary or genetic change is very long. A characteristic period for the emergence of one advanced species from another is perhaps a hundred thousand years. .This evolution constitutes a re-specialization—the adaptation of an organ system originally evolved from one function to another quite different function—which required about ten million years to emerge. The fact that it takes evolution 100,000 or 10 million years to make relatively minor changes in existing structures, shows just how slow evolution really is. The creation of a new species is time consuming indeed. Nevertheless, drastic changes brought about by nature can change the course and the pace of evolution by providing the proper environment.

One such example involves the evolution of mammals. According to one theory, the journey of evolution from birds started around 300 million years ago. The pace of evolution picked up about 65 million years ago as all of the dinosaurs died suddenly and become extinct because of an asteroid strike. The disappearance of the dinosaurs thus leveled the playing field for mammals. Starting with simple mammals, such as the species Didelphodon—a smallish, four-legged creature similar to today's opossum, mammals thrived and differentiated themselves.

In 65 million years, over 4,000 species of mammals evolved from such creatures. According to the Theory of Evolution, random mutations and natural selection produces such diverse species of mammals, ranging from bats to humans. Evolution thus creates thousands of different species, ranging in size and shape from a small bat weighing a few grams to a blue whale that is over 30 meters long and weighs a couple of tons. Humans just happen to be one of these species. At present, the Theory of Evolution or genetic science cannot quite explain the exact sequence of events as to how the human body evolved with all its complexity, from simple organisms or twenty-four basic elements present in a human body.

Scientists are currently busy addressing many of the unanswered questions regarding the present Theory of Evolution.

1.   Coming into existence of the first living cell spontaneously, starting evolution.

2.   The process of modifying genome or adding information to bring about drastic changes, creating complicated organisms.

3.   The coding of the instinct for survival in the DNA

While seeking answers to such questions, scientists might come to a complete understanding of DNA and show how mutations and natural selection explain every part of the development of life on this planet. Alternatively, they might develop a new theory that replaces the current evolution theory and answers the remaining questions. Scientists might even observe, during their research, a completely new phenomenon that accounts for the diversity of life that we see today.

Scientists have been able to come up with several new ideas. They have performed certain interesting experiments to answer various questions related to the Theory of Evolution. We shall discuss these developments further in the last chapter of this book. However, we must remember that the scientists have just finished the task of mapping the human genome. They have just begun their journey to understand life and its evolution at the cellular level.

The DNA molecule in a human cell is indeed complex and includes all sorts of coded information in 3 billion base pairs. Scientists are just beginning to understand some of this code and the function of various genes, proteins and the effects of base pair mutations. For example, scientists are beginning to trace the changes in the sex-related X and Y-chromosomes starting around 300 million years ago. As scientists learn more, the refinement of the scientific theories concerning evolution will continue.

The science related to understanding DNA is in its infancy, and the connections in DNA are indeed extremely complex. According to evolution scientists, it is only fair to give science some time to cope with the complexity of the causal connections. Just because science cannot yet cope with the complexity and explain everything or answer all the questions, one need not take refuge in religious speculations based on mere belief. For example, we should not hastily jump to the conclusion that God created all the species and human body with all its complexity all at once at some point in history. We must at least unveil the process and the sequential steps required for the creation of the human body, which go beyond the simplistic stories advanced by religion.

However, one should not casually dismiss the theory of creation or Intelligent Design, advanced by some religious people. It is, of course, important to examine what religion has to say about the meaning of life, why people believe in religion, and why we have so many religions. In the next chapter, we indulge in this exercise.

Chapter 3
Religion & Mysteries of Life

3.1 *Introduction*

Continuing our journey, we examine and discuss the meaning of life from a religious perspective, tracing its historical origins and delving into the basic beliefs of different religions. The notion of soul, God, and spiritual science is also discussed. Finally, we ask the question: *"Has religion the answers to all questions concerning life?"*

3.2 *Meaning & History of Religion*

We can define religion as a system of beliefs, based on humanity's attempt to explain the universe and natural phenomena. In fact, the English word 'religion' probably originated from the Latin word 'ligare', meaning to bind, to join, or to link. The prefix 'Re-'could be viewed as an intensifier, or mean 'back' or 'again'. Religion, translated literally, would thus mean to strongly bind, bind back, re-join, or re-link; thus binding or joining humans to the so-called Divine. Of course, non-English speaking religions coined their own terms, such as Hindus' Dharma and Moslems' Mazhab.

Religion often involves supernatural forces. It requires its followers to follow certain prescribed religious obligations. Most of the religions attempt to answer the following questions:

- What is God?
- What is the soul and what is its relationship to God?

- What is the soul's relationship to the body, senses, mind, and intellect?
- What is nature and what is its relationship with the soul and 'God?
- What is perceived as good, and what is bad?
- What is the goal of life?
- What happens when death occurs?

Different religions provide different answers, and every religion believes it alone has the right answers. Though different religions provide different answers or differ in sources of authority, they all share several common features. For example, most of them believe in rituals, life after death, code of conduct, and belief in the supernatural. One finds that most of them convey the same basic message and have similar beliefs with minor variations. Each religion believes in some form of God, though each one has its own God—the only true God—and a different path to reach Him.

All religions require faith and they attempt to influence the thoughts and actions of their followers. The beliefs that are common to most of the religions are listed below.

- Belief in a Creator or God
- Belief in creation instead of evolution
- Belief that a soul exists in every human body
- Belief that we are all God's children
- Belief in some kind of existence after death
- Belief in the union with God as the goal of life
- Belief in different paths to achieve this goal
- Beliefs that we should be compassionate; do well.

Some religions consider branches of philosophy, such as metaphysics, separate from religion. For example in ancient Greece, Judaism, and Christianity, they draw a distinct line between metaphysics and religion. On the other hand, Hinduism and Buddhism consider metaphysics and philosophy inseparable from religion. The 'secularism' implies an idea isolated from religion. A Secular idea or organization does not promote any particular religious teaching. Thus, a scientific idea or belief is secular. Secular political parties and secular governments are also examples of secular organizations as opposed to theocratic ones, based on some religions.

- Birth of Religion

Man, soon after he appeared on this planet, became concerned with security from the external world. Through senses, he observed various heavenly bodies in the sky, and sensed the mysterious forces at work on Earth. He saw rivers, mountains, rain, and the oceans. Based mainly on fear, the human mind invented different gods, such as the sun god river god, and rain god, etc. Man came to believe that a supreme power, God, created this universe and everything in it. Religion and the belief in the Creator for the universe provided a simple answer to all the questions. God did it, and he does not have to explain how God did it.

When a natural disaster struck, man often looked towards the sky, prayed, and asked for favors from God. Fearing hunger, wild animals, sickness, and death; coupled with a sense of helplessness, led humanity to invent religion. Man's first instinct was to believe that there was some higher power or authority, which could punish or help him. His mind conjured up illusory beings that could determine or alter the outcome of all the fearful events. He sought to bring these gods on his side and secure their favor by means of magic, prayers, and by offering sacrifices. Thus, religion originated from fear. Some leaders or priests who seek special privileges pretend to mediate between ordinary men and the gods the men fear.

Human fantasy, therefore, created gods in man's own image—gods who could determine and influence various phenomena. Religion continues to evolve through the period of human history. The idea of God in religions today is a refinement of the old concept of the gods. Many religious followers pray to God and ask for the fulfillment of their wishes. Religion extends its domain and looks for the meaning and purpose of life. It seeks answers to the questions such as, *"Who am I?"* and *"Why am I here?"* Whilst seeking these answers, religion

44

creates the concept of an omnipotent God and soul and the linkage between the two.

Spirituality comes into religion as religions preach the concept of soul or spirit and its relationship to God. Some preachers ask humanity to look beyond the material world and seek the meaning of life and death. Most religions preach good conduct, ethics, and moral codes that raise the conscience of humankind through faith and help humanity. However, some leaders with personal stakes involved distort and exploit religion, which leads to violent conflicts and clashes among people of different faiths, even within the same religion.

Different religions started in different parts of the world, based on different faiths and beliefs. With the passage of time, religions have evolved gradually. Various prophets and messengers come and preach various religions, based on their personal experience. They appeal to human emotions, their aspirations, fear, and talk about sin, merit, heaven, hell, morality, and ethics. Surprisingly enough, most of the religions essentially preach similar basic values, ethics and morality, which are important for a smooth functioning society. The Ten Commandments such as, *"Thou shalt not steal, not commit adultery,"* etc., exist in some form in most religions. Various religions also became social institutions once human beings started living in organized societies.

Religion has also evolved with the evolution of science. Science has long been dispelling many wrong religious beliefs concerning various natural phenomena, explaining them in terms of cause-effect governed by the laws of nature. Religion has tried to keep pace with science by raising questions about the complex phenomena that science cannot yet explain. Religious proponents talk about Intelligent Design Theory for the universe and the existence of the Creator, who designed the universe with all its complexity, created the laws of nature, and the universe itself. One cannot ask question as to who created the Creator, because the Causality Principle (suggesting that every effect has a cause, and an effect cannot precede a cause in time), does not apply to God. He was, is, and will always be present—not bound by time, space, and causality.

We have defined the term religion, and given some idea about its origin and its initial purpose. Now, we dig deeper and see how various religions evolved historically. Most religions trace their origin directly from God or gods. They claim to come directly from actions of God or gods and/or their word communicated to the chosen messenger(s). Thus, the exact origin of any particular region is usually controversial.

As previously stated, many scientists including Einstein, non-believers, archeologists and historians think that some form of religion came into existence when man first walked on the planet and stood in fear of nature. The practice of religion was also used by man to comfort, to understand life, to record events and history, and for entertainment. We obtain some idea about humanity's beliefs and practices from early human remains, art, and artifacts.

We find evidence for the religious ideas of early civilizations in elaborate burial practices, such as the creation of the pyramids and tombs in ancient Egypt, and other prehistoric records or monuments. For example, it was common practice to leave valuable objects with the deceased, intended for use in an afterlife or to appease the gods. Tomb paintings also show a belief in life after death. We have no written history but only scattered physical evidence, which is often difficult to interpret.

Institutional religion came into existence in two parts of the world: India and the Middle East. The Aryan/Vedic religion, or Hinduism as it is currently known, originated in India. It was inclusive in that it claimed that all prayers, no matter where they originate, go the same supreme deity—God—known by different names. The sectarian religions; namely, Judaism, Christianity, and Islam, originated in the Middle East. These religions were exclusive in the sense that each of them believed that their God was the only proper God. According to each of these religions, only those who believed in the particular religion went to Heaven.

Most of the organized religions had priests who acted as mediator between humans and God or gods. They occupied positions of power and privilege as they kept the art of writing mostly to themselves. Hinduism, Christianity, and Islam all point to archeological evidence, such as archeological findings, cities and the people mentioned in their early writings of holy books and religious manuscripts. Let us now examine these organized religions, starting with the religions originating in the Middle East.

- Judaism

According to a Jewish scholar, over 4,000 years ago God established a divine covenant with Abraham, making him the patriarch of many nations. Four religions trace their roots back to Abraham: Judaism, Christianity, Islam, and the Baha'i World Faith. The book of Genesis describes the events surrounding the lives of the three patriarchs: Abraham, Isaac, and Jacob. Christians recognize Joseph as a fourth patriarch by Christians, but not by Jews.

Moses was the next leader of the ancient Israelites, who led his people out of captivity in Egypt and received the Law from God. After decades of wandering through the wilderness, Joshua led the tribes into the Promised Land. Samuel converted the original tribal organization into a kingdom with Saul as its first king. The second king, King David, established Jerusalem as the religious and political epicenter. The third king, King Solomon, built the first temple there.

The division of the Northern Kingdom of Israel and the Southern Kingdom of Judah occurred shortly after the death of Solomon in 922 BC. Israel fell to Assyria in 722 BC and Judah fell to the Babylonians in 587 BC. After the destruction of their temple, some Jews returned from captivity under the Babylonians and started to restore the temple in 536 BC. Orthodox Jews date the Babylonian exile from 422 to 352 BC.

Alexander the Great invaded the area in 332 BC, after which Greek became the language of commerce and its culture became a major influence on Judaism. In 63 BC, the Roman Empire took control of Judea and Israel. By the 1st century BC, four major and some minor religious sects had formed the Basusim, Essenes, Pharisees, and Sadducees. Many anticipated the arrival of the Messiah who would drive the Roman invaders out and restore independence.

The Tanakh corresponds with the Jewish scriptures, often referred to as the Old Testament by Christians. It is composed of three groups of books: Torah, Nevi'im, and Ketuvim. The Talmud contains stories, laws, medical knowledge, and debates about moral choices, etc. It is composed of material, which derives mainly from two sources: the Mishnah's and the Gemara. According to many Jewish scholars, the widely accepted minimum requirements of Jewish beliefs are essentially Rambam's thirteen principles of faith, listed below.

1) God exists.
2) God is one and unique.
3) God is incorporeal.
4) God is eternal.
5) Prayer is to be directed to God alone and to no other.
6) The words of the prophets are true.
7) Moses' prophecies are true, and he was the greatest of the prophets.
8) The Written Torah (the first five books of the Bible) and Oral Torah (teachings now contained in the Talmud and other writings) were given to Moses.
9) There will be no other Torah.
10) God knows the thoughts and deeds of men.
11) God will reward the good and punish the wicked.
12) The Messiah will come.
13) The dead will be resurrected.

- Christianity

Christianity tracks fourteen generations from Abraham to David; fourteen generations from King David to Jech-o-ni'as and his brethren carried away to Babylon; and fourteen generations from Babylon to Jesus Christ around 2,000 years ago. Christianity started with Jesus of Nazareth. They believe that Jesus traveled as a preacher and teacher in Palestine. He healed and worked wonders and soon got into trouble with the conservative religious and political forces; therefore, they crucified him. It is believed that he rose from the dead, was resurrected and appeared to many followers who proclaimed him to be God's promised Messiah, or the Christ (in Greek).

Jesus chose twelve disciples, later reduced to eleven because of the treachery of Judas Iscariot. Peter and Paul were the most outstanding preachers. Peter suffered martyrdom under Nero in Rome in 65 A.D. Paul broke with Jewish tradition and spread the new religion to the Gentiles (non-Jews). He was beheaded in Rome about 65 AD. The movement started by Paul flourished and quickly evolved into the religion of Christianity. Christianity continued to spread over the Mediterranean world for 250 years after the martyrdom of Peter and Paul. By 287 AD, it became the state religion of Armenia. The history of Christianity just before Titus' triumph in 70 AD and a century later is uncertain. However, as this period ended, it was flourishing with churches, bishops, clergy, sacraments, and the subtle theology.

The Roman Empire was on the decline in the 2nd and 3rd century. Nevertheless, Diocletian, a Roman emperor, did persecute Christians during his reign from 284 to 305 AD. Soon after this time, Constantine took control and leaned towards Christianity as a unifying force for his multicultural empire. He became a great patron of the church. Christians began fighting each other over certain issues, such as whether Christ was of the same substance as God the Father. . The issue was finally resolved when Constantine presided over a historic meeting of 200 bishops, which declared Christ to be of the same substance.

The history of Christianity from Constantine is uncertain. The Eastern Church was seeking to protect its spirituality through withdrawal from the worldly contacts. Anchorites in Egypt followed extremely ascetic practices to subjugate flesh and cultivate poverty. This ascetic movement established monasteries, and St. Jerome—a notable champion of this movement—translated the Old and New testaments from the original Hebrew and Greek versions into Latin. His version, the Vulgate, is the bible of the Roman Catholic Church today. The Bishops of Rome soon began to exercise civil and ecclesiastical authority, which led to the Papacy.

In 455 AD, the Vandals sacked Rome, and over the course of another two centuries, Moslems conquered Hippo and the other Christian bishoprics in North Africa. Fighting and political anarchy prevailed in Europe for almost a thousand years after the fall of Rome. During this chaos, the Christian Church widened its boundaries. St. Patrick of Ireland also gave women an important role in evangelizing Ireland. However, the institutional authority of the Western Church remained centered with the bishops of Rome. By the end of the 12th century, Popes became so powerful that they could dictate to the kings. In the 7th century, as Islam came out of Arabia, it overran Syria, Egypt, Persia, Palestine, and North Africa. Christians and Moslems fought bitterly in Europe and around the Mediterranean for a thousand years.

In the meantime, the public started questioning the Pope's esteem and authority, and movements for Church reform started in many countries. Peter Waldo founded Protestant churches in Italy four centuries before someone coined the term 'Protestant'—to protest the Pope's authority. Martin Luther came up with his theses, which rejected the prevailing concept of salvation. He claimed that salvation was a gift of God to sinful man, gained by faith in the divine promise that Christ by His atoning death had paid the penalty for sin. This led to the affirmation that the Bible is the sole and sufficient source of Christians' spiritual guidance. This led to the denial of the Pope's infallibility, as a source of doctrine. Such reform movements led to the division of Christianity into two main sects: Roman Catholic and Protestants.

At first, on discovering the New World, the American colonies accepted the European pattern of church establishment. However later on, when the First Amendment to the Federal Constitution was adapted, it barred congress from making any law respecting an establishment of religion. This gave legal status to the principle of the separation of church and state. At present, in the United States and around the world, one might divide Christians into four major branches: Roman Catholic, Protestant, Eastern Orthodox, and Anglican. Protestants divide themselves further into more than 255 sects.

At the same time, there seems to be a disconnect growing between Catholicism and its followers, especially in Western Europe and the United States. According to recent surveys, Catholics follow their own conscience in matters of birth control and several other issues instead of following the Pope, and still consider themselves good Catholics. The Pope and the Catholic Church continue to resist the change. Recent sexual scandals involving clergyman have also damaged the image of the Catholic Church.

Continuing with our journey, the Bible is the only scripture of Christianity and Jesus Christ the only Son of God, who shall come to judge the dead. Christian prayer begins with *"Our Father"* which Jesus first taught in the Sermon on the Mount. Christianity emphasizes the fatherhood of God, and the fact that every human being is God's own child. Christianity also puts more emphasis on having the Lord present here and now. Christianity welcomes all those who will acknowledge Christ and try to follow Him.

One could perhaps summarize the basic beliefs of Christianity as follows. Apostles' Creed expresses most of the beliefs used by most Christians with slight variations. Baptists and Congregationalists do not accept any binding creed. In general, for individual Christians the basic faith is that only God's grace and Christ's life and death can save man.

1. God is the Father Almighty.
2. Jesus Christ was His only Son.
3. Jesus was born of the Virgin Mary, suffered, was crucified, and buried.
4. On the third day, he rose from the dead and ascended into Heaven.
5. Jesus sits on the right hand of God the Father Almighty.
6. Jesus shall come from there to judge the dead.
7. Christians believe in the Holy Ghost, communion of-saints.
8. Christians believe in forgiveness of sins, resurrection of body, and everlasting life.

- Islam

Islam, founded by Prophet Mohammed, is a relatively young religion. Prophet Mohammed was born in 570 AD. His family of the Koreish belonged to the tribe that was responsible for the care of pilgrims and Kaaba, which had the most sacred shrine for Bedouin idolatry. Mohammed was a sensitive and contemplative person and he developed distaste for such idolatry and respect for the Jewish and Christian monotheism. According to the writings, during his meditation and contemplation, the angel Gabriel cried, *"Recite!"* Beginning during Ramadan in 610 AD, he revealed the holy book Koran to Muhammad over a 22-year period. Muhammad believed that he was the prophet of Allah, and Allah is the one and only God.

Mohammed started denouncing the idols merchants from Mecca, who threatened his life. He finally fled to a friendly city, Yathrib, where he became the religious leader and governor. It was later named Medinat an-Nabi (City of the Prophet). After winning the war with Meccans, Mohammed entered Mecca and destroyed all idols in the Kaaba except the sacred meteorite enshrined there; Black Stone. Mohammed died in 632 AD but Islam continued to spread.

Over the next 20 years, Islam spread rapidly to Syria, Iraq, Palestine, Egypt, and the Persian Empire, conquered by the fierce Arab armies. Conquered populations embraced Islam. For Islam, the 9th -11th centuries are called the Golden Age of Islam. During this period art, poetry, philosophy, mathematics, medicine, and architecture flourished. Islam continued to spread as merchants and mystics traveled across Asia, and Arabic armies conquered and moved into India.

Moslems, the followers of Islam, believe that the Koran is God's last and best-preserved revelation to man. It appears that the Koran's approved text was prepared shortly after Mohammed's death by one of his followers. The Koran contains many legends and traditions similar to the Bible and pagan Arabia. All Moslems accept the Koran as the word of God, and it provides the basis of the laws of Islam.

The primary doctrines of Islam are pure monotheism and the Last Judgment. Although Arabs had long accepted the existence of supreme deity, Islam emphasized Allah as the one and only God. Moslems believe that Allah is the sole creator and only judge, the doctrine of Last Judgment. Based on a person's deeds, the person goes to Hell, described as coverings of fire, pestilential winds, and scalding waters, or to Heaven, epitomized by gardens and lovely virgins.

Islam is perhaps the simplest and the most explicit religion. It is still united by the binding force of faith. Moslems all over the world profess the same simple beliefs, utter the same prayers, and turn towards the same holy city. There are some differences, especially over the question of Mohammed's successor, which persists today and splits Moslems into two sects: Sunni and Shia. However, a vast majority of Moslems remains Orthodox Sunni, who do not believe in a successor to Mohammed and keep the religion intact.

Mohammed prescribed the ritual observances, known as the Five Pillars of Islam:

1. Proclamation of the unity of God and belief in Mohammed—the Messenger of Allah
2. Prayers performed five times daily facing Mecca and every Friday in the mosque.
3. Almsgiving, as an offering to Allah and an act of piety
4. The fast of Ramadan
5. Pilgrimage to Mecca

In addition, the Koran also contains certain moral and legal ordinances, which provide the basis for the Islamic way of life. These ordinances prohibit the eating of pork, gambling, the practice of usury, and the making of images depicting Mohammed or God. These ordinances also prescribe rules for marriage and divorce and penalties for crime.

Unfortunately, some Moslems misinterpret some of the teachings of Islam. They believe that it is justified to kill 'kafirs'—those who do not believe in Islam. If they die in 'Jihad' or such a holy war fought for their religion, they become martyrs. Such misguided fanatics have caused many problems for modern civilization by indulging in terrorism, killing innocent civilians in the name of Allah and their religion.

- Hinduism

Hinduism, mostly practiced in India, is perhaps the oldest and most complex religions, but also one of the most tolerant. Many consider Hinduism a philosophy and a way of living rather than a religion. According to Hindu philosophy, people belonging to apparently different religions are, in fact, also Hindus. The most ancient Hindu scripture Rig Veda states: "Truth is one, but the sages speak of it by many names." Thus, a Hindu believes that there are many paths to God. Christianity and Jesus is one path, Islam and Qur'an another, and spiritual practice yet another. They are all equal. No path is better or worse.

According to western historians, the Aryans introduced this religion when they migrated to India several thousand years ago. Debris recovered from a recently discovered site, including construction material, pottery, sections of walls, beads, sculpture, and human bones and teeth; has been carbon dated and found to be nearly 9,500 years old. India's National Institute of Ocean Technology recently discovered a city on this site—five miles long and two miles wide—underwater in the Gulf of Cambay off the West coast of India, and identified huge geometrical structures at a depth of 120 feet.

The civilization uncovered appears to be more ancient than the pyramids in Egypt. The BBC reporter Housden, reporting on this find, said that we would have to remake from scratch the whole model of the origins of civilization. If additional research were able to identify that the culture of the city's inhabitants is that of the Vedic people, it would radically change the whole picture of Indian history written by western archaeologists.

Hinduism has a vast variety of scriptures mostly written in Sanskrit language, the mother of most modern languages. According to Hindus, their primary scriptures, Vedas comes directly from God. Numerous sages meditating about God realized the absolute truth and they passed on their findings to their disciples. These disciples inscribed these teachings on leaves and later on paper. Other scriptures include Srutis or Upanishads (the condensed version of Vedas, Smritis, or Dharma shastra) stating the proper way of life for a normal person; Puranas, and epics supporting Dharma shastras by narrating several anecdotes and stories.

All of these scriptures essentially express the same truth in different ways. They all convey the same message to different people at different levels. The Srutis clarify that there is absolutely no difference between various scriptures. Bhagavad-Gita, one of the most important and popular scriptures of Hinduism, describes the essence of Hinduism. Einstein praised this Hindu scripture. He said that everything else seemed superfluous, when he read Bhagavad Gita and reflected on how God created this universe. .

Hinduism permits all points of view, and it has no problem accepting the teachings of most of the religions. The central belief in Hindu philosophy or religion is that there is only one supreme soul— God, and God has no religion. Human beings label themselves with different religions and give God different names. Just as different rivers known by different names, lose their individual identity when they finally merge into an ocean. Similarly, with individuals who, when labeled with different religions lose their identity, their souls merge and dissolve into the supreme soul. A Hindu scripture thus states that the whole world is just one family, and all prayers reach the same Creator (God) irrespective of where they originate.

Hindus have historically welcomed many different religions currently practiced in India. Hinduism has also given birth to several great religions, such as Buddhism, Jainism, and Sikhism. Hinduism accepts and respects these and all other religions. In fact, Hindu majority in the world's largest democracy in India has recently elected a Moslem President and a Sikh Prime Minister for the country.

Hinduism encompasses all of the noble principles of other religions. According to the theoretical physicist Professor Brown, who has translated Upanishads into English, Hindu philosophy appeals to scientists because the emerging scientific picture of the universe is very close to the Hindu's cosmic view. Although Hinduism has included many apparently divergent views, we can state the central belief as follows.

The first shloka in Isha Upnishad neatly sums up the Vedanta philosophy of Hinduism. In Sanskrit language, it states, "Isha vasyam idam sarvam yat kincha jagaryan jagat" meaning that God permeates every living being and inanimate object. In other words, Vedanta philosophy emphasizes the 'Oneness of God', and states that we must see God in everyone and everything, and see everyone and everything established in God. God exists within us and the ultimate goal of life is self-realization. Our soul is on a journey, is potentially divine, and can become one with God once it realizes itself. Some of the tenets of Hinduism, assembled from various scriptures, are as follows.

- Soul & God
Soul has the following attributes:
a)   The soul' is a conscious field confined within the body.
b)   The soul identifies with nature, is bonded to it, and it enjoys the world through the senses and mind.
c)   The goal of the soul is to disentangle itself from nature, free itself from bondage, and reunite with the super-conscious field—God.

God has the following attributes.
a)   God is unconfined, unbound, unaffected, infinite, a super-conscious field with unlimited intelligence.
b)   God permeates and influences all animate and inanimate objects in this Universe.
c)   God is beyond space, time, causation and thus beyond our limited body senses, mind, and intellect.
d)   God is immeasurable, can manifest in many forms, but can only be known by direct experience.

- Body, Mind, & 'Soul'
The relationship of soul to the various elements of the body is as follows.
a)   The mind receives signals about the worldly objects through physical senses.

b) The mind interprets and evaluates these signals according to the acquired values.

c) The bonded soul enjoys or suffers in this world according to the reactions of the mind.

- Nature & Soul

Nature or the outside elements of the universe surrounding the body affect life, as follows.

a) Nature produces all the motion and stability, etc. in this universe according to set laws.

b) The soul's bondage to the body is caused by nature.

c) Nature attracts the mind, intellect, and soul, and causes a reaction.

d) Nature and God are without beginning. God creates nature, nurtures it, and then destroys it, starting the cycle again

- The Body's Action & Reaction

a) Our nature and acquired values govern our behavior.

b) We interact with nature through physical senses.

c) Our intellect evaluates data based on our acquired values.

d) We react after the interpretation and evaluation of the data.

e) God does not plan our actions or the fruits of our actions; but nature and our values do.

f) One can change values through proper religious practice.

- Purpose of Life & Religious Practices

a) The purpose of life is self-realization and the reunion of soul (conscious field) with God (super-conscious field).

b) The self-realization process has four steps: renunciation, purity of mind, devotion, love of God and humanity.

c) Renunciation implies detachment from worldly desires and from the fruits of our actions. Meditation helps detach the mind from the world and nature.

d) Purification of the mind implies its control, directing it towards God—difficult but possible.

e) Devotion implies developing a close relationship with God.

f) Love of God and humanity implies a sincere love for God, serving humanity.

Thus, Hinduism defines spiritual self-realization and the union with God as the purpose and goal of life. It has the premise that 'Soul' moves through many lives seeking to merge with God, like a river reaching out to sea and losing its own identity. To achieve this self-realization goal, Hinduism suggests four paths, namely; selfless action, the pursuit of truth through knowledge, devotion, and meditation, described below. Hinduism allows people the freedom to follow any religion or path that suits their basic nature.

- Four Paths

1. Selfless Action (Karma Yoga) -Provides efficiency enabling the soul to reach God through selfless service and duty. It is more suitable for action-oriented characters.

2. Knowledge (Gyan Yoga) -Sharpens intellect, enabling the soul to reach God by knowing the absolute truth. It is more suitable for intellectuals.

3. Devotion (Bhakti Yoga) -Unifies one in a relationship with a personal God, enabling the soul to reach God. It is more suitable for emotional and sentimental characters.

4. Meditation (Raj Yoga) -Purifies the mind, enabling the 'Soul' to reach God by going beyond the mind and intellect. It is more suitable for characters who are more easily detached from the world.

It proclaims that all the paths listed above converge, merge, and lead to the same destination—the realization of God. Selfless action leads to renunciation, renunciation to purity of mind, true knowledge to devotion, devotion to love for God and humanity; leading finally to God. Hinduism thus gives personal freedom to choose one's own path, means and methods and even a personal God to achieve the same goal. Because of the personal choice, the several symbols, stories concerning God, deities, and scriptures are used. Other religions and those who have not studied the religion often misunderstand and ridicule these symbols.

- Buddhism

Continuing our visit, we briefly discuss another great religion. Buddhism is in fact an offspring of Hinduism. Siddhartha Gautama Buddha, born around 563 BC into a Hindu royal family in Lumbini, was raised as a prince. One day, when he stepped out of the palace, he saw an old man, a sick man, a dead man, and an ascetic. He was deeply affected by the human suffering and decided to leave the palace and became a monk. At the age of 29, he started his journey to seek the solution to human misery, trying various forms of meditation. Finally, sitting under a Bo tree in a city Gaya, India, and meditating for 49 days, he achieved Enlightenment. He preached his first sermon in the city of Banaras (Kashi) in India on the bank of river Ganges. He then traveled for 45 years, preaching and converting people to Buddhism.

Buddha, born as a Hindu, accepted many concepts of Hinduism such as the doctrine of Karma, Ahimsa or nonviolence, and the need to release one's soul from worldly desires, but he disagreed about the methods to achieve the result. Buddha—the originator of Buddhism—proposed the doctrine of the following four noble truths:

a)   Existence of suffering in cyclic existence
b)   Cause of this suffering
c)   Cessation of suffering
d)   The path resulting in the cessation of suffering

According to Buddha, 'self' or the soul is not a part of the supreme soul, as Hindus proclaim. It is an impermanent state of mind undergoing continual change. One can get rid of worldly desires; the cause of all human misery, and achieve true self-realization, leading to Nirvana—the discovery of the final truth and release from the Wheel of Rebirth. Although any person can practice this religion, a Buddhist monk must have three essentials: poverty, nonviolence, and celibacy.

To achieve the intended goal, Buddha proposed a Noble Eight-fold Path, which is an antidote to the state of suffering existing in cyclic existence. The Eight-fold path suggests a certain mode of attitude, thought and action. It comprises of the following components:

1) Right knowledge
2) Right Intention
3) Right Speech
4) Right Conduct
5) Right Livelihood
6) Right Effort
7) Right Mindfulness
8) Right Meditation

The great emperor Asoka, ruling India during 269-237 BC, made Buddhism the state religion. Buddhist monks spread Buddhism as they traveled to many Asian countries including China and Japan. Over the centuries, Buddhism has diverged into almost two different religions: Hinayan Buddhism of South East Asia and Mahayana Buddhism of Northeast Asia. Both sects do accept Buddha as the embodiment of a principle of enlightenment, but they have different views regarding the practice of religion.

- Some Other Religions

There are several other religions with a limited number of followers, such as, Jainism and Sikhism. Jainism was born in 6 BC as a revolt against some of the Hindu practices. Jainism did keep many of the Hindu practices. Its main teaching is Ahimsa; nonviolence in any form. Its goal of life, like Hindus, is to seek liberation of the soul from the cycle of rebirth. Another great religion originating from Hinduism is Sikhism. Around 1500 AD, Guru Nanak founded the Sikh religion in India and compiled the Sikh scriptures. Nine generations of gurus succeeded Guru Nanak. Guru Granth Sahib is the main scripture.

There are also the Parsees, who fled to India from the conquerors of Persia. Parsees are the followers of Zoroaster, the Persian religious genius who lived around 6 BC and expressed his opposition to any deity worship in human form. Finally, there is the Shinto religion in China—"the Ways of the Gods"—that essentially involves quiet worship in shrines and before ancestral tablets. This draws on a Confucian influence that evolved from early Japanese animistic rites. Confucianism and Taoism, founded by Confucius and Lao Tzu in China, are not religions in the normal sense. Both of these founders were great philosophers whose teachings are quite illusive and intangible. Another religion not so well known is Sufism. Its great proponent was Jalalludin Rumi, who said that love is the astrolabe to the mysteries of the universe..

As discussed above, several religions came into existence throughout human history. It is amazingly clear that all the major religions, although initially appearing diverse, essentially have unity of purpose. They convey the same key message with different words. In fact, they are all trying to reach the same God, described by different names and symbols. They follow the paths shown by Messiah, Jesus, Prophet Mohammed, or Hindu sages. Hindus already believe that these are different paths lead to the same goal. However, many people from different faiths find it difficult to realize this unity or believe in a universal religion with their faiths forming the branches of the same tree.

People can have different opinions, follow their own convictions and faith, and yet see unity in diversity. Most religions convey the message of peace, love, and compassion, although sometimes, the practice might differ from the actual preaching of the religion.

History also shows that religions, when misinterpreted and practiced improperly, have caused a great deal of bloodshed and human misery due to their explosive emotional appeal. On the other hand, religions have helped humanity and uplifted the spirit when they preach the message of love and compassion and strive for the noble goals. Religious tolerance is the key to achieving these goals. Unfortunately, some religions are exclusive and intolerant.

- Classifying Religions

One can classify religions in many ways based on many criteria, such as their historical origins and the characteristic answers, they provide for various concerns. These concerns relate to the nature of God or gods, our purpose on Earth, goals in this life, preparing for and experiencing the afterlife, and our relation with the divine. Different religions also refer to different sources or authority. For example, we can also classify religions in the following manner, according to the nature of the referred authority.

1) Monotheistic religions—worship only one deity and usually have doctrines and a professional priesthood. Examples include Christianity, Islam, Judaism, Sikhism, and the Baha'i faith.

2) Polytheistic religions—worship many deities; with each deity considered a separate entity. Examples include the mythologies of ancient Greece and Egypt, ancient Rome, and the Vikings, etc.

3) Shamanistic religions—worship ancestors or spirits rather than gods and are typically limited to small geographical areas.

4) Pantheistic or "natural" religions—see everything in nature as an aspect of a spiritual plane. Such faiths include Shinto's and several animistic traditions.

5) Other religions (also called spiritual philosophies)—focus more on teachings towards achieving self-realization and true happiness. Examples include Buddhism, Hinduism, Taoism, and Confucianism.

Note that Islam and Judaism are monotheistic. Christianity believes in only one God although it does develop a notion of God as one in three (the Father, Son and Holy Spirit), as explained in the doctrine of the Holy Trinity. The Baha'i faith is also monotheistic, which says that several major world religions all originate with God. We group all the polytheistic religions under the heading of mythology. Mythology consists of religious stories and beliefs. In sociology, however, the term myth means stories which are important for a group and which could be true.

Of course, the classification of religions into monotheistic and polytheistic faiths presents difficulties for religions that include spirituality as an integral part of its teachings. Such classification obscures the true nature of religions such as Hinduism and Buddhism. Hinduism essentially believes that all is ultimately one, although it has many gods and goddesses. Various gods, goddesses and even religious institutions, according to Hindu philosophy, represent different facets of the single truth.

According to Hinduism, various deities are projections of One Reality, which is beyond the perception of the human mind. Furthermore, different paths can lead to the same destination or the ultimate truth. Hinduism prescribes various paths; e.g., devotion, action, knowledge, and meditation, to find the ultimate truth. Hinduism accepts other religions as different paths to achieve the same absolute truth. Buddhism declines to comment on the nature of ultimate reality or non-reality.

- Why People believe in Religion?

There are several reasons for belief in a religion. For some, it is the search for simple answers for the creation of life and the universe. For others, it is the search for a higher purpose for human life and the desire for some sort of continuity in the afterlife.

There are different types of believers in every religion. Some people simply enjoy visiting churches or temples. Others like to study religious scriptures. There are also those who consider themselves deeply involved with the Divine. They may reject much of the recognized aspects of established religion. Many people may not accept extreme religious practices, such as some punishments under Sharia law or the historical burning of heretics. They find such practices repugnant to the secular ethics of a modern liberal democracy. Various reasons for the continued belief in religion are as follows.

1) Moral- Religion provides proper moral and spiritual values through childhood education.

2) Fulfillment- Religious practices such as meditation and Yoga bring peace, happiness, and fulfillment.

3) Emotional- Religion provides practices that cause an emotional high; from the singing of traditional hymns or the trance-like states experienced through worship..

4) Supernatural- A reality that includes the supernatural belief in life after death and eternal life

5) Authority- The authoritarian nature and spiritual and moral role models have positive influences on society.

6) Traditional- The practice and effect of traditional ceremonies appear majestic and reassuring.

7) Cultural- Many secular-minded individuals follow religion for cultural reasons, for the continuation of traditions, and for family unity.

8) Community- Religion promotes a sense of community, provides social, and support networks.

9) Intellectual- Intellectual evaluation concludes that a particular religion describes reality.

10) Life Purpose- Religious teachings show followers the real purpose of human life.

- Why People do not believe in Religion?

Belief in religion has been on the decline recently in much of the developed world. The development of science, rational thought, and increased prosperity has made people critical of religious beliefs and, therefore, has alienated many people from the mainstream religions. Many people also seek spiritual satisfaction outside of organized religion. Some of the reasons for non-believers not following religion are as follows.

1) Intolerance—Religion hurts society by promoting intolerance between people of different faiths.

2) Harmful—Some religions enforce their version of 'God's Law' through governments, causing misery.

3) Unsuitable morality—Simplistic and narrow religious morality adversely affects the ability to deal with real-world problems with no real God to assist.

4) Unappealing practices—Religious practices and ceremonies appear pointless and repetitive.

5) Restrictive -.Religious practices are too restrictive, prohibiting prosperity, enjoyment, and pleasure.

6) Self-promoting—Religion enables certain individuals to grab and abuse positions of power and privilege.

7) Irrational and unbelievable—Many disagree with the religious interpretations of ethics, human purpose, and views of creation.

8) Contradicting 'common sense'—Religious views of nature, supernatural, or the afterlife goes against common sense.

9) Promoting ignorance—Early education in religion is akin to brainwashing, promoting ignorance at a young age.

10) Mind dulling—Religion dulls the mind and gives false hope, hindering people from dealing with reality.

3.3 *Religious Meaning of Life, Soul, and God*

We briefly visit and address some very controversial topics in this section. These topics are also examined in detail in the last chapter.

- What is Life?

Almost every religion starts with the premise that a soul resides in every human body. Life derives its meaning from the soul, and human life cannot exist without a soul. Almost all religions also believe in some kind of post existence for the soul after death. Most religions promise its followers that if they lead their lives according to the dictate of their particular religion, their souls will enjoy a good afterlife.

Hinduism also believes in the pre-existence of soul before birth. It advances the Theory of Karma, which says that our past decides our present; and our present decides our future. The cycle of Karma for a soul extends to pre-existence, current existence and post-existence. They believe that since there is a cause for every effect we observe in this universe, there must be a cause for what happens to us in life.

According to most religions, soul is an essential element of life, a part of the supreme soul—God. Most of the religions believe in creation instead of evolution, and believe that God directly created man and woman. However, every religion presents a different story regarding the creation of life. Most religions simply do not accept the Theory of Evolution.

- What is Soul?

As stated, almost every religion believes in the existence of a soul inside the body. The concept of soul evolved gradually. Initially, the human mind was concerned with security from the external world. Through the physical senses, it looked at the various heavenly bodies in the sky, and sensed mysterious forces at work on earth as it gazed at the rivers, mountains, rain, and the oceans. The human mind invented different gods for the phenomena it could not understand—sun god, river god, rain god, etc. Many of these gods faded away as science later gave a rational explanation for these natural phenomena.

While analyzing the external world, the human mind turned its attention inwards to analyze human life. Man observed that everything in the outside world kept changing and that nothing was permanent. He started asking questions about the human life. Is there anything permanent about human life? What distinguishes the dead from the living? Is there anything that does not die with the body? If so, what is it, where does it come from, and where does it go after death? The concept of the soul was thus born in the human mind. It was quite appealing, because it promised the continuity of life. It also gave meaning to human existence.

As per other religions the Hindu religion also believes in the existence of soul but it considers it a part of the Supreme Soul—God. It states that the body is not 'I'. Our ego; a self-image of oneself is also not 'I'. 'I' is the sole driver of our bodies. The soul, spirit, or consciousness is like energy. Since energy can neither be created nor destroyed, the soul is never born and it never dies. The body decays and dies. All souls are on a journey through different human body experiences, are part of one entity, and are potentially divine.

Spiritualists believe that soul comprises conscious energy, which expresses itself through thoughts, intellect, and stored values or impressions. According to some, consciousness is everything that we know and do not know. At conscious level, it makes us aware of we see, hear, touch, eat, drink, and feel. It helps us deal with people, places, world at large, and even with birth and death. At subconscious level, it is the flow of life energy (prana) which makes us breathe, digest, and maintain the balance of bodily metabolism, cellular and hormone level growth and regeneration. At super conscious level, it is the collective essence of memory and life experiences, and the discriminative mind.

Thus, soul or consciousness gives us identity, ego, and makes us what we are. Many spiritualists also believe that there is a continuous flow between the conscious, subconscious, super conscious, and even the supra conscious.

According to some spiritualists, its seat is at the intersection of the line from the forehead to the back of the head, and the line running across the top center of the brain. It functions with a thought based on stored impressions as we observe the universe; intellect then analyzes it, discriminates, and sends a signal to the brain to react in a certain manner. The cycle continues—thought, discrimination by intellect, and re-enforcement or change in stored values, belief system, or impressions.

According to Hindu scriptures, Vedanta, souls become imperfect due to their bondage to Karma, and the goal of life is to break this bondage and realize their potential divinity. On death, the body is left behind and the soul, accompanied by the life force (of Prana), goes in search of a body where it can further its goals. It thus keeps on moving through various lives, until it realizes itself, becomes pure bliss, and merges with God.

Some people with near death experiences narrate strange happenings when they survive death. They claim to experience light and a journey to strange places. Skeptical scientists call it a delusion of the mind, instead of a journey of the soul, when the supply of oxygen and blood flow is reduced to the brain at the time of death. Regarding the journey of soul through pre- and after-life, some quote the instances when people can describe places from a past life, which they have never visited in the present life, under deep hypnosis. One American woman on a TV show claimed that on waking up one day, she suddenly started speaking fluent German, when she had never learned a word of that language.

- What is God?

Most religions agree that God is the ultimate Creator of our universe and life. Different religions describe different qualities of God. For example, they agree that He is benevolent, kind and loving, and takes care of His children. Hindu scriptures such as "Vajra Upanishad and Patanjali Sutra go further and characterize God as unique indwelling omnipresence that is never tainted nor touched by the actions and reactions which afflict ignorant individuals.

God is what is left over after the ego-ignorance-collapse, that special inner ruler or intelligence, which is unconditioned by time and whose will alone prevails even in the body. There is a sense of oneness that is never divided. It is therefore beyond ignorance and its progeny. Another Hindu scripture Bhagavad-Gita states that God is everywhere, inside and outside everybody and every entity; He is subtle and hard to understand; He is close and yet very far. In short, God is infinite, and words are inadequate to describe Him.

3.4 *Spirituality—Life, Soul, and God*

With developments in science, increased rational thinking, and disillusionment with organized religion, many people nowadays prefer to describe their beliefs as spirituality rather than religion. This trend represents a movement towards an increasingly modern, rational, tolerant, and intuitive form of religion. Eastern religion has always viewed spirituality as part of the religion. Moderating movements can now be witnessed within religions such as Christianity and Islam, etc. Even scientists are getting in on the act, trying to inject scientific inquiry and spirituality into religion.

It seems strange that in each religion, one prays to God, but the followers of each religion think that their God, with a specific name, belongs only to their religion and is different from other that God of other religions. More than half of the population on this planet does not pray to a Christian, Moslem, or Hindu God. Most of them have not even heard all the different names of God. The followers of each religion think that they are the chosen ones who will enjoy heaven, and that others are doomed to live in hell.

Obviously, any sensible person would not want the majority of our planet's population to burn in the fires of hell. Could it be that all religions are actually praying to the same God unbound by any particular religion? Hinduism already believes in this concept and considers the world as one family, with all prayers going to the same Creator.

Eastern religions consider spirituality an integral part of religion. Indian religions: Hinduism, Buddhism, Sikhism, and Jainism have always woven a primary focus on spirituality into their core framework. Hinduism calls its Vedanta philosophy, related to the human soul, the spiritual science in contrast with the material science that is related to matter. It claims that the science looks outwards at the material world and discovers the laws of nature that govern the material world. Science thus explains the presence of matter, energy, and primitive life in the universe, and seeks the answer to the question: *"Where am I?"*

Spirituality, on the other hand, looks inwards inside our mind to seek the answer to the question: *"Who am I?"* It attempts to define the word 'I'. Hinduism also places emphasis on the potential divinity of man and sets the goal of life to know oneself. Many spiritualists believe in the existence of soul inside a body. The innate quality of the soul is happiness and purity. However, because of the actions performed by the body, it is intertwined with all of the 'sanskars' or values that we accumulate. These values are continually modified and stored as pattern in our mind, resulting from our actions, reactions, and interactions with the outside world.

According to spiritualists, the goal of life is to achieve self-awareness, self-realization, and awakening of the inner self. They say that everything that happens in life is like a scene in a drama and we are acting a role. Thus, we must realize that every situation or scene is temporary, as the situation will change, and therefore our role is temporary. The only eternal element is the actor, oneself, or 'I'. Furthermore, as an actor and a director, one does not have to follow a prescribed script—the 'I' in all of us controls thinking, perception, and actions in a given situation. The 'I' in all of us can also be creative and change behavior or role without having to react negatively to any situation.

Once a spiritualist learns the notion of detachment as an actor acting out a scene, no situation in life can bring misery. One can remain detached, and yet be sensitive to the suffering of others. The essence of spirituality is to know and to love the inner self. One can love others only after one learns to love one's own inner self.

Love requires that the constant nurturing of virtue, respect, and dignity for oneself. Virtue includes compassion, positive feelings, self-respect, detachment, and not reacting to a negative situation in a negative manner. Once our inner self cultivates virtue, we can play a loving role in every situation, even if others do not respond lovingly. One must focus on one's own journey, and not worry about how others react to that journey.

Many spiritualists also believe that the sense of 'I'" is a peaceful and happy soul. This soul is on a long journey through many lives and it is part of the supreme soul. They believe in the law of Karma or action; namely, you have to face the consequences of your actions in any life.

Spirituality teaches one to achieve potential divinity; a union or merger with the Divine like a river merging into the ocean and losing its own identity. God—the supreme power or energy—permeates everything and everybody. It points to a cosmic conscious field that is beyond intellect; not bound by space, time, and causality. One can only experience God by getting away from the material world and focusing internally.

The tools used to experience this supreme power are very different from laboratory apparatus. Such tools are again subjective. They provide the means to observe the internal state and analyze our own mind, our feelings, and our actions. According to Hindu philosophy, yogic or transcendental meditation is the most powerful tool to rewire our values, change our behavior, and experience God.

- Spirituality and Yoga

Yoga is often misunderstood in the western world as mere physical exercises, yet it literary means union. The practice of Yoga in Hindu philosophy is more than physical exercises (Asana) for the body. It is an extremely detailed, rational, and so-called scientific approach to developing the body, mind, and soul. The ultimate objective is to realize the spiritual truth; namely union with the Divine. Raj Yoga prescribes an eight-fold path or eight-step ladder to achieve union with the Divine. Patanjali in Yoga Sutra considers the first five steps; grouped together as 'Samyama', as the preliminary foundations of Yoga. These steps lead to the trio—Dharana, Dhyana, and Samadhi—the ultimate goal of Yoga.

The eight steps are as follows.

1) Yama—the code of conduct used to resist the inclination towards immoral behavior (injunctions akin to the Ten Commandments).

2) Niyama—rules for cultivating cleanliness of the body and mind, alongside contentment, austerity, or control of senses, self-discipline, self-study, and surrender to the Divine Will.

3) Asana—physical Yoga exercises to keep the body healthy and in perfect posture, supporting the ability to invoke divine life energy.

4) Prayanama—control of the life force (Prana)—A link between physical matter and the spirit to awaken the cosmic energy within in body, caused by Prana, through the breathing process.

5) Pratihara—the withdrawal of the mind from the outward sensory perceptions and letting it explore the inner supreme existence.

6) Dharana—intense concentration, fixing the mind on an inner or external object of meditation to reprogram our values, and to reach the higher state of divine consciousness.

7) Dhyana—meditation, focusing of the free spirit and realization of its external nature; omnipresent within and beyond all creation.

8) Samadhi—the super-conscious state involving full realization bereft of ego or , thoughts; losing sense of space, time and causality; becoming one with the soul; and communion or merger with the Cosmic Spirit, God, or Sat-Chit-Ananda (eternal, conscious, and blissful).

According to Supreme Yoga, the universe is a mere reflection in consciousness, like scenery reflected in a crystal ball. However, such a reflection does not affect the true consciousness. Jiva (soul) is the vehicle of consciousness and intelligence of the ego-sense is its vehicle.

Prana is the life force or energy of the mind and our senses. Prana coupled with motion (action or Karma) is the body's own vehicle towards fulfillment.

The type and range of senses limits our perception of the scenery of the observed universe. All perception arises in consciousness, exists, and then dissolves within consciousness. Thus, consciousness is the true reality. Our body is just an inert mass but for Prana and the mind. The true or unconditioned consciousness is the supreme self (soul). This supreme self ordains both mind and Prana to promote life in the body. The mind goes wherever Prana takes it. When the mind is submerged in the supreme, Prana ceases to move, and thus the mind achieves a quiescent state. This, in essence, is the basis of meditation and self-realization through Yoga.

- Spiritual Science

Spiritual sages claim that the body of knowledge about spiritualism is indeed science. In Hindus' Vedanta philosophy, they claim that just as science starts with the perception of certain facts, so does true religion. For example, we accept the law of gravity as a perceived fact verifiable by independent observation. Reasoning is comparison with a perceived fact, and other deductions follow from this fact. There can be no reasoning without perceived facts. Thus, all knowledge arises from the perception of certain facts (laws) through our reasoning.

In a similar manner, spiritual scientists argue that the acceptance of God is a perceived fact. No arguments can prove or disprove this perceived fact; namely, the existence of God. Regarding the verification of this fact, they argue that just as one can verify the existence of gravity, so can one verify the existence of God. However, the tools for the verification of this fact reside within us, and not in a science laboratory. They are subjective and not objective as in science. Unfortunately, several religions ask the human mind to believe their dogma and accept it as perceived fact.

Just as some believe that soul is pure energy, many spiritualists believe that God is also a source of intense pure energy. Thus, they believe that since energy can neither be destroyed nor created, souls and God are eternal. In other words, God was always there, and souls never die. With the passage of time in the material world, everything drifts towards increasing disorder from perfect order, according to the second law of thermodynamics, and the unusable energy increases with decreasing usable energy. Similarly, in the living world souls drift from a perfect state of peace and happiness into a chaotic state. According to spiritualists, eventually the ultimate source of Energy—God—intervenes and restarts the whole cycle for the universe and the life contained within it.

According to one sect of spiritualists, Brahamkumaris, using proper spiritual tools that reflect inwards, anyone can realize and experience the perceived fact—God. They characterize soul as a point of light residing in our body and God as an intense source of light that illuminates all souls. According to them, God resides in a region that is not bound by time and space. That region was also the abode of all souls before they came to this world, and all these souls will eventually return to God. In fact, they say that one can visit the abode of God as often as one likes through the practice of meditation.

This process starts with the mind creating the initial thought to visit God. Intellect then creates a picture of God's abode from that thought—a far-away place in the universe. The soul residing within us then leaves the body and begins the journey into outer space. It spends some time in outer space before returning to the body. As we discuss in the next chapter, this is another practice of meditation based on visualization.

According to the Vedanta philosophy, God is within each individual. Only those who go beyond joy and misery, good and bad, virtue and vice, being and non-being, can realize God through the power of introspection.

One can provide the following analogies for describing the relationship and nature of the soul and God. The first set claims to be a reflection of God.

1. Just as the same Sun reflects from the water filled in different pots, the same supreme soul (God) is reflected from different bodies.

2. Just as the images of the Sun, seen in different water-filled pots are distorted because of environmental interference, the souls in the bodies are affected by nature and Karma.

3. Just as the different distorted reflections of the Sun are images, different souls in bodies bound to nature are bonded souls (Jivatmas).

4. Just as the quality of different images can improve by adjusting the medium and pots' bottom surface, the bonded souls (Jivatmas) can improve by adjusting their interaction with nature.

5. Just as different images can be poor, average, and good; different bonded souls (jivatmas) can be as tamsik (evil), rajas (worldly), or satvik (noble).

6. Just as one has to make an effort to improve an image from a pot, one must make an effort to purify or self-realize each soul.

7. Just as the process of cleaning images involve several steps; the process of self-realization of soul (jivatma) involves detachment from worldly desires, purity of mind, change to Satvik values, and freedom from bondage.

8. Just as images in only a very few pots get to be perfect, only a few souls are purified and shine like the supreme soul.

9. Just as a perfect image from a pot shines like the Sun, a bonded soul (jivatma), when completely purified (self-realized) and free from bondage, shines like the supreme soul.

10. Just as image from the pot once perfected does not require further adjustments, a soul (jivatma) once completely free and self-realized does not struggle anymore, and becomes one with the supreme soul—God.

The second set of analogies presents the same concept in a slightly different form.

1. Just as different pots fill up with the same air, different bodies fill up with souls (jivatmas), part of the same supreme soul—God.

2. Just as we cannot see but only experience the air inside or outside the pot, we cannot see but only experience the soul or the supreme soul—God.

3. Just as the quality of air in a pot depends on the pot's environment, the quality of soul (jivatma) depends on the acquired values (samskaras).

4. Just as we characterize the air quality in a pot as clean, average, or dirty, similarly we can characterize a soul (jivatma) as Satvik, Rajasik, or Tamasik. It applies to human nature or the body's actions.

5. Just as the air inside a pot, when cleaned by a process becomes the same as the outside pure air, the soul in a body, purified through a process, becomes a self-realized soul (Atma) and one with the supreme soul—God.

6. Just as it requires efforts to clean the air inside the pot, it takes efforts to purify the soul (jivatma) inside a body for self-realization and merger with the supreme soul—God.

7. Just as the process of cleaning air inside a pot may involve several steps the process of soul (jivatma) purification or self-realization involves various steps: change to Satvik values, detachment from worldly desires, purity of mind, and finally freedom from bondage to nature.

8. Just as air from a broken pot can migrate to another new pot, a soul (jivatma) can migrate from one body to another body on death and continue the struggle for purification or self-realization.

9. Just as one must help clean the air inside every pot to clean the entire environment, one must help purify or

self-realize each soul (jivatma) for union with the supreme soul—God.

10.   Just as air in only a few pots becomes clean in practice,
only a few souls (jivatmas) purify and merge with the
supreme soul.

3.5   *Does Religion have the Answers?*

Religion, obviously, does not have all the answers except for the
believers who do not want to ask questions. Although religion offers
answers to many questions concerning life, it does not appeal to many
people especially the younger generation with scientific thinking. Answers offered by religion are unacceptable to them simply because they
are speculative, based on mere belief. We cannot verify them independently and experimentally, and thus it is difficult to subject them to
the methods of scientific inquiry.

Spiritual science has some appeal for the younger generation
since it introduces some objectivity into religion. However, despite
spirituality, the age-old problem related to human ego remains.
Whether a religion does or does not include spiritual philosophy, its
followers might be intolerant of other religions since they claim to
have attained superior understanding. Followers of each religion usually philosophize to prove that they are right and others are wrong.

We must remember that religion consists of a set of beliefs and
belief, after all, is just a belief. We must learn to respect beliefs that are
different from our own but, unfortunately, such is not the case. This
has led to a lot of bloodshed and untold misery in the name of religion.
Organized religions are not doing a good job of uniting humanity on
this planet. In fact, evangelical fever and fanaticism is on the rise, causing untold misery in the world.

Obviously, it does not make sense that only one religion has the
exclusive rights to Heaven, if Heaven exists. If it were true, it would
imply that only people following that particular religion would go to

Heaven and non-believers would go to Hell. There are good and bad people in every religion, and God should not punish good people just because they did not worship Him in a certain way.

We must be hopeful that in the future humanity moves away from such narrow thinking and religions develop a more tolerant approach by embracing spiritual science components within their teachings.

Chapter 4
Frontiers & Top Ten Mysteries of Life

4.1 Introduction

In this phase of our journey, we explore the frontiers of life. Firstly, we focus on the most important tool that gives us the power to analyze. We observe that our brain sets us apart from all other species. We then revisit genetics and the evolution of culture, including the optimum Universal Principle of Change, in particular how it has affected the evolution of life on this planet. The top ten mysteries of life are also listed before we look inside our crystal ball and predict the future.

4.2 Frontiers of Life

To learn about any object in nature, we need a source to 'illuminate' the object with some field. Then we need sensors to perceive the field affected by the presence of the object. The brain processes and integrates the data from the sensors; it projects our personality and gives meaning to life. It also sets us apart from other species. Understanding the brain is critical for understanding the truth about life.

The brain is part of the nervous system that controls and integrates the activities of all parts of the human body. It collects, processes, and responds to information. It is only through the processing of data by the brain that we learn about life. Several mysteries remain about the brain. Some of these include questions concerning the processes associated with dreams, sleep, biological clock, memory storage, and access; and the impact of genes and the environment on our thoughts, personalities, aging, and consciousness, etc. Our brain generates the feelings of spirituality and faith in God. Therefore, the first stop during this phase of the journey is the human brain.

Our brain receives information from senses, associates it with past patterns stored in memory, processes it, uses an optimality criterion according the values of a particular individual taking into account the constraints; and then formulates the most appropriate decision and plan of action. It also associates feelings and emotions with the received information. In short, it is the most complex computer.

Despite intense research efforts, for example at Microsoft, by scientists from all over the world including Eric Horvitz, we still do not have a complete understanding of how the human brain functions. A brain institute funded by software billionaire Paul Allen claimed, in 2006, that it had completed a map of the mouse brain down to details of individual cells. Work is also already beginning on a similar map for the human brain. To unfold the mysteries of the brain, we need to make substantial progress in several areas.

In August 2006, scientists discovered a gene called HAR1 that had undergone accelerated evolutionary change in humans and was active during a critical stage in brain development. Scientists at the University of California, Santa Cruz compared genes from humans, chimpanzees, and other animals to see what sets man apart. The evidence suggests that HARI may play a role in the development of the cerebral cortex, and may help to explain the dramatic expansion of this part of the brain during human evolution.

-The Human Brain

In order to find out more about the functions of the human brain, we need to examine its complex thinking process. We shall also observe how these functions make us intellectually superior than the other species. Obviously, the power of our brain and it is the ability to perform various functions is limited and varies from person to person.

Recent advances in biological research appear somewhat promising in gaining an initial understanding of the natural thinking mechanism.

- The Brain's Structure

The brain is part of the nervous system. It controls and integrates the activities of all parts of our body. It collects, processes, and responds to information. The nervous system is divided into the Central Nervous System (CNS) and Peripheral Nervous System (PNS). The CNS is composed of the brain and spinal cord, has both sensory, and motor neuron cells. The PNS is composed of 12 pairs of cranial nerves connected to the brain, and 31 pairs of spinal nerves connected to the spinal cord.

Several sketches of human brain are given in Fig. 4.1 (courtesy of NIH).

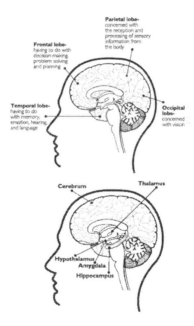

Fig. 4.1—Human Brain

The brain is enclosed within the cranium, which is contained inside the scalp connected to skin. The outer part of cerebrum is composed of gray matter made up of nerve cell bodies and the interior part is composed of white matter, which consists of axons forming pathways and ventricles filled with cerebrospinal fluid. The cerebrum controls speech, memory, and intelligence. The Prefrontal cortex stores working memory.

The brain also has cerebellum, located under cerebrum, which controls and coordinates certain subconscious activities. It has a brain stem (medulla, pons, mid-brain), which connects the spinal cord to the brain and maintains breathing. It has a hypothalamus, the endocrine regulatory center, which influences our sleep, appetite, and sexual desire. It also has thalamus, a critical relay station linking the cerebrum to all parts of the nervous system.

- Neuron Cell—Key Element

The essential element of the human brain is the neuron cell. We originally believed that the body could not generate new neurons because we assumed that these cells provided us with the ability to remember, think, and apply previous experiences to our every action. However, according to latest research, neuron cells do regenerate. Although we do not yet know the factors controlling neuron-genesis, the generation rate and new connections do increase with a moderate amount of regular physical and mental exercise. A neuron has several components, such as dendrite, axons, etc.

Each neuron axon is connected at the button at the end of axon to other neurons across a small gap called a synapse.It receives inputs, combines, performs nonlinear operations, and sends outputs to other cells/ neurons. It conveys information via electrochemical pathways and essentially consists of standard cell bodies and processes. The dendrites bring inputs through synopsis that are processed over time, and transmits the output through axons to other cells. The dendrites, which are short and tree-like with branches, can receive and transmit impulses to the cell body. The axons are long with fewer branches that carry impulses away from the cell body at a small gap called the synaptic gap.

The strength and polarity of the new input signal is determined by the physical and neurochemical characteristics of each synapse. A neuron's dendrite tree is connected to a large number of neurons. When such a neuron fires, a positive or negative charge is received by one of the dendrites. The strengths of all the received charges as inputs are added together through the processes of spatial and temporal summation. Spatial summation occurs when several weak signals are converted into a single large one, while the temporal summation converts a rapid series of weak pulses from one source into one large signal.

The aggregate input is then passed to the soma (cell body). The part of the soma concerned with the signal processing is the axon hillock. When the aggregate input exceeds the axon hillock's threshold value, the neuron fires and transmits an output signal down the axon. The strength of the output signal is constant, and its value is not affected by the strength of the input signal as long as it is greater than the threshold. The output strength is also unaffected by the many divisions in the axon, and it reaches each terminal button with the same intensity it started with at the axon hillock. Schwann and satellite cells in PNS and neuroglia in CNS form a fat-like substance (Myelin) to provide an electrical insulation sheath surrounding certain segments of axons listed below.

- Unipolar—one process axon/ dendrite; e.g. sensory neurons in peripheral nerves.
- Bipolar—axon and dendrite; e.g. in the retina and inner ear.
- Multi-polar—one axon and more dendrites; e.g. motor neurons in the spinal cord transmit impulses to muscles and glands.

There are two types of neurons: sensory and motor, which are structural and functional units of the nervous system. There are over one hundred different classes of neurons depending on the classification method used. Individual neurons are complicated. They have a myriad of parts, sub-systems, and control mechanisms. They convey information via a host of electrochemical pathways. About 100 billion neurons can connect with up to 200,000 other neurons, although connection with 1,000-10,000 neurons is typical.

The power of the human mind comes from the sheer numbers of these basic components and the multiple connections between them. It also comes from genetic programming and learning. Together, these neurons and their connections form a process, which is neither binary, nor stable, nor synchronous. In short, it is nothing like the electronic computers currently available or even the artificial neural networks.

The signaling mechanisms that wire up the 100 billion cells in the human brain are also not fully understood. A few thousand genes in the human genome tell 100 billion neurons to wire themselves precisely in the human brain. We do not understand how so few genes can meticulously wire so many neurons. DNA and various genes in it seem to have special properties that make the brain function more efficiently.

- How does our Brain Work?

Recent advances in biological research appear somewhat promising in terms of gaining an initial understanding of the natural thinking mechanism. The basic functions performed by our brain are illustrated in Fig. 4.2 and discussed one-by-one below.

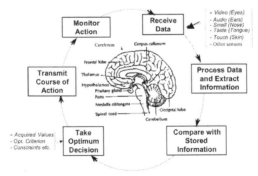

Fig.4.2—The Thinking Process of the Human Brain

For the brain to think and decide on a course of action, it needs to perform these basic functions as it interacts with the outside world.

- The Brain receives Data

We start our journey by visiting our body senses, since we use our senses to interact with the physical world. All inner experiences consist of reproductions and combinations of sensory impressions. The human brain receives and coordinates visual-, audio-, smell-, taste- and touch-data received from the multiple sensors, eyes, ears, nose, tongue, and skin, respectively.

Our body sensors have achieved a fair degree of sophistication during genetic evolution. For example, our eyes are far more sophisticated in many ways than any camera. The eyes can take a stereo dynamic picture and transmit the signals continuously to the brain in real-time through the optical nerve. According to current estimates, the eye transmits data through the optical nerve at roughly 10 million bits per second. An Ethernet connection transmits information between computers at speeds of 10 million to 100 million bits per second.

Man has invented many sensors, which emulate our senses and even go beyond them. Many of these man-built sensors have a wider frequency range and better resolution than our body sensors. We have built video, audio, touch and other sensors, etc.; however, these sensors in many ways cannot surpass the performance of body senses. The audio sensors, for example, cannot discriminate between signals in the same frequency range as well as ears do. The human ear has the exceptional ability to pick up one particular conversation when several people are talking in the same frequency range.

- The Brain Processes Data

As soon as our senses carry data about an event to the brain, it is processed. The extracted information is stored as patterns in a distributed memory through neuron connections. Research confirms that the human brain stores the extracted information as patterns. All of the acquired knowledge and skills that we have ever learned are stored into the neural network in our brain as memories. This makes each of us unique and it gives continuity to our lives. To understand anything, it is essential to understand how memories are stored in the brain.

On receiving new information, the brain triggers an initial search and neurons make connections, recalling previously stored patterns corresponding to previous events that are even remotely related or associated with the current event. The process involves recalling and evaluating the observed patterns, utilizing the stored patterns and then solving problems. It involves the creation of massive parallel networks and the training of these networks to solve specific problems. It might even use fuzzy logic and not just a simple 'yes' or 'no' (1 or 0) binary bits. It uses vocabulary that is very different from traditional computing, and uses words such as behave, react, self-organize, learn, generalize, and forget.

- The Brain Takes the Optimum Decision

What distinguishes man from an animal? An animal's brain cannot process the amount of information that the human brain can. Moreover, an animal's brain is more hardwired and does not have as much flexibility to continuously make new connections and take far-reaching decisions as the human brain does. Recent findings suggest that some animals are also capable of planning for future events. For example, according to researchers, a male chimpanzee in a Swedish zoo planned hundreds of stone-throwing attacks on zoo visitors. Recent studies at the University of Illinois show that the part of the human brain involved with memory and decision-making can be increased and the neural strengthened, simply by walking or doing mental exercises.

Most of our behavior is the result of processing information and taking conscious decisions based on certain optimality criteria. In other words, the human brain starts collecting and processing a huge amount of information. It then finds and implements the optimum course for the set objectives. It does not seem to follow the path of least resistance or random changes to adapt to the changes.

During the process of decision-making, connections are continuously made as various options are considered. Most of these connections are discarded after initial evaluation, using the existing constraints and the optimality criterion based on the stored values. The brain focuses on the remaining few connections that pass this test. These connections develop further, connecting to other stored patterns that relate to events, embedded in the stored patterns.

These patterns can rapidly become complicated. An example would be the decision making process by the brain to recognize a face. The eyes carry the face's image signals from many different angles to the brain. The brain extracts the critical features, compares it with the stored patterns, uses an optimality criterion, and comes up with the final decision concerning the recognition of the individual face.

- The Brain Transmits a Course of Action

Having decided upon an action, based on intelligent analysis and optimality criterion according to its values, the brain implements the action. The required signals are transmitted to the corresponding parts of the body that take the necessary action to implement the decision. The transmission of the desired signals through the nervous system is the key.

- The Brain Monitors Action

To monitor the action and achieve the intended results, the cycle of sensing the data, processing and extracting information, comparing with the stored patterns, modifying the decision if needed, and transmitting the modified signal continues. The process stops only when the intended result is achieved. Alternatively, the brain, on observing the outcome, decides to drop further action on the selected task.

Do animals have the same capability as human beings? The recent finding of an infant gorilla in a Congo sanctuary smashing palm nuts between two rocks to extract oil; is surprising and intriguing scientists. Another gorilla crossing a river went back to pick up a stick to find out the depth of water. Scientists say that we have much to learn about what gorillas can do—and about the implications for evolution.

- The Brain Controls

Our brain is the master controller in the body directing various activities. How does it affect our health, mood, and our values? An organism's genome encodes proteins. These proteins perform most of the activities that we associate with life; directing cells to grow, communicate, reproduce, and even die.

Approximately 35,000 genes are responsible for almost everything that happens inside our body. They make the proteins in our bones, the enzymes that digest our food, the hormones that control our reproduction, and the chemicals that govern our moods, thoughts, behavior, and personalities. The human body is an incredibly complex chemical factory that produces all sorts of chemicals. The maintenance of good health is directly linked to the chemical balance in the body.

The balance in the body is directed by the signals from the mind. In fact, the actions directed by our mind; based on the processed data according to the acquired patterns, define our personality. Such actions by the mind can also generate different chemicals that dictate our mood and feelings of pain and pleasure.

Our actions can bring about a chemical imbalance in the body that can lead to or accentuate several diseases. Our energy levels and health also depend on the efficiency of the processes inside our bodies that transform. For example, food transforms into energy; produce the required elements, and transport them. Through the signals transmitted by the nervous system, the produced chemicals give the feeling of pain or pleasure.

For example, everyone seeks happiness but happiness is a state of the mind, which can be brought about by different chemicals that control our moods. Our body is capable of producing chemicals like dopamine that is released in the nucleus accumbens and frontal cortex in the brain. This dopamine floods the synaptic gap between nerve endings and binds to receptors on the adjacent cells, thus activating more neurons involved in memory and emotion, generating a feeling of pleasure. Neurons also release chemicals such as opioids/endorphins to numb pain or prevent the pain signals from reaching nearby cells. This produces a feeling of pleasure or euphoria elsewhere in the brain.

Drugs can create an artificial high. Narcotics mimic opioids, cocaine triggers the release of dopamine, and alcohol and nicotine affect both dopamine and endorphin circuits, producing a feeling of euphoria. However, such drugs interfere with the natural trigger mechanisms for dopamine and endorphins and repeated use can fool the brain into craving those drugs, leading to addiction. People altering the state of their minds through chemicals or drugs get high and experience, through delusion, a reality far different from the conventional reality. Most of these mind-altering drugs are harmful and highly addictive.

- The Brain & Consciousness

Many scientists, including neurobiologists, believe that awareness or consciousness is simply a neurobiological physical process arising through the structure and dynamics of the brain. They have shown, through MRI and ECG studies of the brain; that many subjective experiences such as perception and sensation occur due to changes in the chemical processes of the brain. Science has not yet undertaken a serious study of consciousness. They are busy mapping various parts of the brain and studying its dynamics.

Spiritualists' and Buddhists' concept of consciousness is very different. They question the assumption that consciousness is simply an emergent property of the matter inside the brain. They believe that matter and consciousness are very different, and matter cannot reduce to consciousness. Buddhists have developed an elaborate methodology to study the subjective experience and consciousness itself. They use the mind of an individual in to analyze the subjective experience of the consciousness. Thus, the mind is the observer, the object of the investigation, and the means of the investigation, unlike objective scientific experiments where the observer, object, and means of investigation are separate. The mental technique is called meditation.

- Meditation & Mind

Meditation, derived from a Latin word, literally means healing. We usually think of meditation as a means to make a restless mind calm, quiet, balanced, alert, and attentive. Instead of using drugs a monk, through meditation, can create a blissful state or 'tranquility' of mind. However, in Buddhist philosophy, meditation means much more than a relaxation technique. They consider it a powerful technique to cultivate mindfulness, focus the mind sharply on an object or concept for analysis, and to direct the attention to any chosen object or concept, whilst keeping the mind tranquil and pliant.

The second stage of meditation, called Vipashiyana, enables us to gain insight through applying a focused beam of analysis and, at the same time, keeping the balance between mindfulness, attention, focus, and tranquility. Meditation, considered part of Raj Yoga, enables our mind to regain control over our actions. It is perhaps the only tool used to reprogram our mind and our values. It enables us to change our outlook and look at different situations positively to help us react accordingly.

Ancient Hindu and Buddhist scriptures describe different meditation techniques. For example, Bhagavad-Gita describes a number of techniques that have minor differences. Some strive to make the mind bereft of any thought; some focus the mind on an object, and others encourage the visualization of a pleasant environment or even God. A monk in such a state of mind feels bliss or true happiness, and even claims to experience the true reality of the universe.

Meditation usually begins with the passive observation of breathing in and out. It leads to observing the inward link between the mind and the body through our sense organs, which make us aware of the world around us. At first, it appears a hopeless task, but with practice, one can train the mind just as one would train a wild horse and bring it to the desired state, bereft of any thought. It stops thinking of the past, present, and future.

One such technique teaches how to observe passively body sensations or subtle vibrations as one learns to scan the nervous system, after blocking out other mental activities. One may experience strange sensations as the nervous system resonates. Another technique practiced by spiritualists, encourages the mind to visualize a peaceful and serene state, get away from worldly thoughts, and connect with the supreme power—God.

Simply put, a normal meditation technique usually involves the following steps.

- Breathe in and breathe out normally.
- Relax any tightness in the head.
- Open and expand the mind.
- If the mind wanders off, let it go first.
- Relax the tightness again.
- Feel the mind expand and become calm.
- Redirect attention gently back to the breathing.
- Keep the mind calm, not focusing on any object.

Some people also practice concentration meditation, when they focus their mind on the object of meditation. This practice, if not followed correctly, has a tendency to tighten the mind.

Scientifically speaking, meditation techniques affect neural activity in different parts of the brain. It might reduce neural activity by not receiving, processing or reacting to the information from the senses. Studies at Harvard have shown that meditation can essentially deactivate the frontal areas of the brain that receive and process sensory information. Meditation also lowers the activity in the parietal lobe, which processes the information about our surrounding orientation in time and space. It also reduces the flow of incoming information to the thalamus in the brain. Studies at the University of Wisconsin also show that meditation shifts activity in the prefrontal cortex located right behind our foreheads, from the right hemisphere to the left inside the brain. This makes one feel more relaxed and happy.

When we take into account all the scientific evidence, it appears that one could experience bliss or spirituality by controlling the activity in our brains. According to Lutz in the November 2006 online issue of *The Proceedings of the National Academy of Science*, researchers found that monks well trained in Buddhist meditation technique, showed significant differences when compared to those who have never practiced meditation. They showed greater brain activity in areas associated with learning and happiness These results suggest that long-term mental training, such as Buddhist meditation, may prompt both short- and long-term changes in brain activity and function.

Some eastern sages proclaim that the only door to experience true reality or God is through meditation. During meditation, one can voluntarily cease the transmission of data from the senses and stop the mind from thinking about the past, present, or future and from dreaming. According to these sages, God is beyond the mind, time, and space, and not subject to change due to causation. They claim that since science is mainly concerned with causation in time and space that binds the material universe together, it cannot properly address the questions about the existence of God.

Meditation affects the brain. Some people practicing meditation also claim that they can experience God once they succeed in going beyond the mind and intellect. Numerous sages in ancient India described experiences of when the mind loses sense of time and space. The soul is thus believed to merge with the supreme soul—God—losing its individual identity, just as droplets of water merging with an ocean do.

Obviously, skeptics do not believe in God and call such practices delusions of the mind. Scientists might claim that bringing the brain to a certain state through meditational practice has very little to do with experiencing God. One could perhaps bring the brain to this state by tinkering with certain elements within the brain, and religion has no connection with this exercise.

For example, if we cut food intake, the liver supplies energy to the brain lasting approximately 24 hours. After this period, cells start breaking down body fats and protein, which bring about changes in blood composition, hormones, and neurotransmitters, etc. These changes affect the brain and can induce a feeling of light-headedness. Similarly, reducing the supply of oxygen to the brain also affects it profoundly. The brain scan of a meditating person claiming to experience God simply shows that certain parts of the brain undergo changes. Scientists would dispute the claim that it implies the presence of God.

According to my personal experience, whether one believes in God or not, most of the meditation techniques, practiced properly, do relax the mind and make it calm, collected, focused, and attentive. It stabilizes the mind like stabilizing the waves in an ocean. It gives us a feeling of bliss and happiness. Science and religion both agree with this, but not on the interpretation that it is connected directly with God.

- The Brain & Reality

Our view of reality is limited because of the limited range of sensors. Our senses perceive only part of the reality depending on their range. For example, our eye fails to see over 90% of its target. Furthermore, the shape of our eye-lens decides the shape of objects that we see. According to medical science, our brain processing capacity is limited and we use a mere 4% of its total capacity. Ants', cats', or dogs' perception of reality is very different from ours because their sensors have a different range. We receive only a partial view of the whole reality.

What is the absolute reality of the universe, irrespective of the observer and limitations of the sensors used to measure the reality in space and time? The Vedanta philosophy of Hinduism states that the physical world around us is an illusion of our senses. We perceive different scenes within the limitations of our senses, and react to them according to the program or our values stored in our mind. In the ultimate sense, the physical matter we see is a manifestation of energy, and energy can only be experienced but not seen.

- The Brain's Learning Ability & Plasticity

Understanding the biological structure of neurons, their learning ability, and their functioning is critical if we are to develop computers that can think like the human brain. This research shows that the brain stores information as patterns. These connections and patterns are continuously updated. Let us briefly consider the thinking process that the brain goes through when our senses carry information to the brain about an event. The brain triggers an initial search and neurons make connections recalling previously stored patterns, corresponding to the previous events that are even remotely related to or associated with the current event.

We discard most of these connections after initial evaluation, using the existing constraints and the optimality criterion, based on the stored values. The brain focuses on the remaining few connections that pass this test, and develop these connections further. It connects to other stored patterns that relate to events, embedded in the stored patterns. These patterns rapidly become complex. For example, when we see a face, the eyes carry the face image signals from many different angles to the brain, which helps it to recognize the individual face.

The latest research shows that one can generate new neurons and new connections inside the brain during an entire lifespan. The learning ability of the brain can deteriorate or improve, or it can become more or less plastic, depending on what we do with it as we grow. We observe that strong motivational efforts for learning interesting new skills, such as languages, musical instruments, and games, and a moderate amount of physical exercise adds to the plasticity of the brain. On the other hand, not using our brain and not learning new skills makes the brain less plastic, and it starts to degenerate.

- Evolution & Genetics

Scientists are currently pursuing two areas of research to answer the following questions. How does a chromosome duplicate itself? How does a single cell differentiate and ensure that that it develops into a complete human body with everything ending up in the right place?

Scientists have discovered the so-called 'jumping gene', which can move or copy itself from one chromosome to another. According to the book *Molecular Biology of the Cell,* transposable elements have also contributed to genome diversity in another way. When two transposable elements, recognized by the same site-specific recombination enzyme, integrate into neighboring chromosomal sites, the DNA between them can become subject to transposition. Since this provides a particularly effective pathway for duplication, such elements can help to create new genes.

Another area of research involves polyploidy, a process common in plants that can have as many as 100 chromosomes. Through the process of polyploidy, the total number of chromosomes can double, or a single chromosome can duplicate itself.

Another related problem that science cannot resolve is as follows. Modern man is assumed to have evolved from Homo ergaster, present on earth around 2 million years ago as indicated by fossil evidence. The fossil records of the Homo ergaster skull indicate that his brain was half the size of modern man, which is around 1500 cc and packs around 100 billion neuron cells. In other words, our skull and brain doubled in size in the timeline of 2 million years, adding 50 billion neurons. Did it happen gradually in a linear manner or through abrupt changes during those 2 million years? A slow linear increase would require the additional wiring of 250,000 neurons in every child born every 10 years (assuming reproduction every 10 years).

According to the book *Molecular Biology of the Cell*, a comparison of humans and monkeys shows that their cytochrome-c molecules differ in about 1% and their hemoglobin in about 4% percent of their amino acid positions. Humans, distinctive from the great apes, have existed for only a few million years.

Thus, each human gene has had the chance to accumulate relatively few nucleotide changes since our inception, and natural selection eliminates most of these. It would seem that a great deal of our genetic heritage formed long before Homo sapiens appeared, during the evolution of mammals (about 300 million years ago) and even earlier.

The proteins of mammals as varied as whales and humans are very similar. The evolutionary changes that have produced such striking morphological differences must involve relatively few changes in molecules, which make us what we are. These morphological differences might also arise from differences in the temporal and spatial pattern of gene expression during embryonic development, which then determine the size, shape and other characteristics of the adult. In short, there are not that many differences in the DNA of a human and a whale, yet humans and whales look very different. It would appear that small collections of DNA mutations could have a very big effect on the outcome.

Scientists have also shown through some experiments that a tiny change in a single gene can have very large effect on a species. For example, scientists could increase the size of a mouse's brain by 50% by modifying a single mouse gene. They do not know whether mice with an enlarged brain became smarter, and the increased cells were properly connected over this short period.

In another study, scientists showed that even a minimal change in an amino acid on a single gene has a profound effect on speech processing in humans. However, the current Theory of Evolution cannot show or predict how point mutation in a human DNA can add and properly wire a large number of neurons. As we understand these mechanisms, the effects of DNA mutations during development will become clear.

A new animal or a human starts life as a single cell. That cell divides, differentiates and the process eventually leads to the development of an animal or human being. A tremendous amount of signaling must happen between cells during the development process to ensure that everything ends up in the right place. Small changes in these signaling processes can have very large effects on the resulting animal. Scientists are also looking at the effect of small changes in DNA patterns during embryonic development.

Our DNA correctly creates and wires up millions of cells every minute in a developing fetus in the womb. Thus, through a complex process the human genome, with several thousand genes, is able to create a human body. This human body contains trillions of cells, billions of carefully wired neurons and hundreds of different cell types, forming organs as diverse as the heart and the eyes.

We do not understand the signaling mechanisms that wire up the 100 billion cells in the human brain. A few thousand genes in the human genome tell 100 billion neurons to wire themselves with precision in the human brain. We do not understand how so few genes can meticulously wire so many neurons. DNA and various genes in it seem to have special properties that make evolution work more efficiently.

David Baltimore, a noble laureate in medicine, added to our understanding of information flow in the cells. He showed that just as information flows from DNA to RNA to make proteins, information also flows from virus to RNA and DNA, changing the code in the DNA molecule.

Scientists have completed the Human Genome Project, and they are busy determining the genome sequence of many other organisms. For example, the recently completed chimpanzee genetic blueprint—the result of a multi-million-dollar effort involving 67 researchers from the United States, Israel, Italy, Germany, and Spain—has provided important clues for understanding our own biology. According to Robert Waterston at the University of Washington, 96% of our DNA sequences are identical. More intriguingly, the other 4% seem to contain clues as to how we became different from our closest relatives in the animal kingdom.

According to researchers, these results confirmed the common evolutionary origin of humans and chimpanzees. Out of the 3 billion base pairs in the DNA coding for chimpanzees and humans, about 35 million show single-base differences, and another 5 million DNA sites are different because of insertions or deletions of genetic code. Waterston estimates that about 1 million of those coding changes are responsible for the functional differences between humans and chimpanzees.

- Natural Selection and Schema

Darwin proposed the Theory of Evolution in 1850 when we knew so little about cell chemistry and DNA, etc. There is a great deal of controversy regarding its application to the evolution of man from small organisms. Obviously, we cannot completely answer several questions at this point. We are still learning more about the effect of mutations on DNA and about living cells. Darwin's Principle of Natural Selection for evolution is all about the natural selection and incremental changes at the genetic level.

Noble Laureate Murray Gell-Mann advances the notion of complex adaptive systems, which can characterize the complex biological system, evolution system, and immune system, etc. He defines the complex adaptive system as one that takes in information, finds certain kinds of regularities, and compresses them into a schema. Through that schema, the system can describe a certain kind of reality including itself, predict, and prescribe behavior in the real world. Circumstances in the real world exert selection pressure back on this schema. A DNA molecule is an example of a schema. Thus, complex adaptive systems involve selection and variation. At the heart of selection is variation or change. This variation is considered random in the evolution process.

We cannot describe all types of evolutions in terms of schema. Stellar and galactic evolutions take place through some kind of fluctuations or variations. However, there is no evidence yet that this evolution is a complex adaptive system such as life, directed by some kind of schema. We know that a tree grows from a seed—a schema. It has to be a tree belonging to the family the seed came from. However, it will not have the same shape or branches as the trees from the same family due to random environmental variations. Similarly, one might speculate that a schema similar to a seed could lead to the evolution of the universe, subject to random variations.

- Cultural Evolution

Over the past two centuries, we ushered in a remarkable technological revolution, harnessed natural resources, and built machines, nuclear weapons, computers and satellites, etc. This evolution is certainly not genetic. The genetic evolution proceeds at a very slow pace over generations. We have not evolved with genetic evolution alone. The progress we have made during a relatively short geological time can only be attributed to the cultural evolution. This cultural evolution relates to the genetic evolution of our brain and is perhaps more important than the genetic evolution. The usual genetic evolution proceeds at a very slow pace over generations, but the cultural evolution takes place at a rapid pace, thus accelerating the process of evolution.

What distinguishes us from animals is the culture. It is not that animals do not have culture, but their cultural evolution is restricted because their brain cannot process the amount of information that the human brain can process. Moreover, their brain is more hardwired and does not have as much flexibility to make new connections continuously far-reaching decisions like the human brain. The human brain has the ability to make new connections and learn from the information processed by it. It is this ability to make optimum decisions that is directly responsible for the fast cultural evolution. This evolution sets humanity apart from the animal kingdom.

After our ancestors climbed down from the trees, nothing significant happened for a very long time. Genetically, our genome is almost 99% identical to chimpanzees even today. Genetic evolution has changed our DNA from each other by a mere 0.1% over such a long period. If we go back in time, we find that nothing significant happened in our evolution until some Homo sapiens decided to move out of Africa about 50,000 years ago.

As Homo sapiens moved from one continent to another, strange things began to happen as their brain developed the ability to process information more effectively so that they could make better decisions. These decisions do not just consider survival at any cost, but also add other higher values to the optimality criterion. Thus, Homo sapiens began to develop language syntax and learnt to develop better tools, to cultivate, to write and print, etc. Their brain learnt to process information more effectively enabling them to take optimum decisions. The human cultural evolution has indeed accelerated the pace of our evolution since the dawn of the industrial age.

When white people from the west moved to Australia not long ago, they had two options: wait for the slow genetic evolution to change their skin color to adjust to the sunlight, or start wearing hats. They chose the second option based on cultural evolution instead of waiting for the genetic evolution. Cultural evolution also plays a major role in governing all aspects of our behavior. Genetic evolution alone does not govern nor hardwire our behavior. Our behavior is also the result of processing information and taking conscious decisions, based on certain optimality criteria. If our genes governed all aspects of our behavior, Siamese twins would have displayed identical behavior.

In fact, scientists discovered recently that our brains are still evolving. A Chicago team recently compared modern man with our ancestors of 37,000 years ago, and discovered big changes in two genes linked to brain size. According to the team, one of the new variants emerged only 5,800 years ago, but it is now present in 30% of today's humans.

As they told *Science Magazine*, this is very short in evolutionary terms, suggesting intense selection pressures. Each gene variant emerged around the same time as the advent of so-called 'cultural' behaviors. This is a very significant finding. When combined with the Optimal Universal Principle of Change, discussed in the next chapter, it provides an explanation for the rapid pace of evolution in recent periods.

In fact, the microcephalin variant appeared along with the emergence of traits such as art and music, religious practices and sophisticated tool-making techniques, which date back to about 50,000 years ago. It is now present in about 70% of humans alive today. The other variant ASPM originated at a time that coincides with the spread of agriculture, settled cities, and the first record of written language.

Dr Bruce Lahn of the Chicago team posed the big question: did this genetic evolution, seen in the brain, actually cause the cultural evolution of humans, or was it merely by chance? They believe that it relates to the important role that these genes play in brain size. According to Lahn, this evolution of the brain does not necessarily imply we are any smarter, but their studies indicate that the trend is still ongoing, which defines the characteristic of human evolution—the growth of brain size and its complexity.

- General (Optimum) Universal Principle of Change

It is obvious that human evolution was not just genetic, linear, and based on simple criterion. Nature's genetic evolution and all its laws of physics use the principle of taking the path of least action or minimum work (or energy or resistance). However, somewhere along the path of evolution as the human brain evolved, we changed the path of least resistance towards the more complex criterion of optimality. Using a different optimality criterion, based on accumulated learning and values and subject to certain constraints; the human brain could process information more efficiently and yield results better and faster. The brain thus finds and implements the best or optimum course for the set objectives, and not the path of least resistance to adapt to the changes.

The cultural evolution is based on a slightly more general Universal Principle of Change (UPC). As stated earlier, the General Universal Principle of Change uses a dynamic optimality criterion, which is different from the path of least action or resistance. To understand this process, let us first define the term optimality criterion. In modern control theory, when we talk about optimum control systems we talk about the optimality criteria, based on certain objectives.

In fact, most modern control systems use some kind of optimality criterion. It may be the minimum expenditure of energy for satellite maneuvering because fuel is a scarce and a valuable commodity on a satellite. For a missile, it may be the minimal time required to hit the target accurately. On the other hand, it may be the minimum cost or maximum returns (or both) for a business model (or vice versa for a bureaucratic government organization). It could even be a combination of several criteria.

While selecting an optimality criterion, we must also remember that a system is always subject to some constraints. Usually for a given system with certain constraints, we must first define an objective that the system must achieve. Then, we select the optimality criterion within the prescribed constraints to achieve the objective in the best possible manner. This determines the optimum control action to achieve the desired objective. For designing optimum control systems, we use several types of optimality criteria and methods, such as Pontryagin's Principle, and Bellman's Dynamic Programming, etc.

Based on my teaching experience in this area, we can state that the underlying ideas are simple, though the design of optimum control systems requires advanced mathematics. For example, the core of Bellman's Dynamic Programming is the principle of optimality: do the best you can in terms of the chosen optimality criterion from wherever you are under the given constraints. The associated mathematics with this simple principle becomes quite complex, and its implementation runs into the 'curse of dimensionality' problem. The most powerful computers fail to process the exponentially increasing number of options that one must consider at different stages of the multi-stage decision process.

Fabricated physical systems as well as human beings are often subject to unforeseen or random changes. These changes can be either in the characteristics of a physical system to be controlled or in the environment. We design adaptive optimal control systems to meet the challenges due to random variations, using additional control loops for continuous system identification and learning about the changes.

In cultural evolution, the human brain must have used similar concepts to handle random variations. We can modify the Universal Principle of Change to explain the cultural evolution. We include in it the constraints and an optimality criterion, used by the living entities that can process information and make intelligent decisions based on the results of such processing. Different optimality criteria, using different sets of acquired values for selection, have led to the evolution of different societies with different traits and behavioral patterns pursuing different objectives. Finally, this modified optimum Universal Principle of Change also seems to be responsible for governing changes in our behavior and daily life.

- Life & General Universal Principle of Change

Let us illustrate how this modified optimum universal principle governs changes in our daily life. Nobody likes change except perhaps a baby with wet diaper. The reason for resisting change is simple. Change requires effort on our part to adjust to the new environment.

What is our natural reaction to change in the environment? The immediate reaction is to ignore or resist the change without taking any visible action. We become stressed as the imbalance caused by the environment exerts continuous pressure on our mind. When the stress exceeds a person's threshold, they try to make a minor incremental change that requires minimal effort and does not take them too far from the current state of equilibrium.

In other words, most of us first try to follow the path of least resistance. After such minor adjustment, we might feel comfortable for a while, but further variations in the environment usually force us to exert some effort again to readjust. Such incremental changes can go on. It is the main cause of continuous stress in our life. One sees the universal principle of change at work with changes in the environment for which one finds new equilibrium, using the principle of least resistance.

People who panic or freeze and do not follow any course of action to adjust to the change in our environment have mental/physical breakdowns, or perish through heart attacks or through some other disease triggered by stress. Even failure—be it in inanimate objects or in living entities—occurs according to the universal principle of change affecting the weakest link in the body. It is very similar to the failure of a rock sample. Suppose we confine a cylindrical sample of rock in the tri-axial test cell, and increase the compressive loading on the ends to break or fail it. It would continually search for the plane of weakness that requires least effort to fail along that plane.

An inanimate object cannot decide on a course of action based on an optimality criterion other than the path of least resistance. It does not have multiple choices for action. However, a living person does have multiple choices for action. In fact, the cultural evolution has given us the luxury of multiple choices.

A person can thus bring about changes in life by selecting the optimum course of action, based on a different optimality criterion than the path of least resistance. For example if the change in environment becomes too much, a 'smart' person resorts to a path other than the principle of least resistance. Of course, the optimum course of action for different people may not be same for the same situation.

Just like a fabricated physical system, one can usually get to any goal from any state in more than one way. One could even determine the optimum or best path according to the chosen optimality criterion, just as one can find the optimum control action for a system or a process to be controlled.

However, it is important to set the proper goal, realize one's initial state and physical and moral constraints, choose the proper optimality criterion, and put into action the necessary effort or control to achieve the desired goal. Every individual has the personal freedom to set goals in life, and can strive to achieve these goals through one's actions based on one's values and constraints.

- Society & General Universal Principle

The General Universal Principle of Change, when applied properly to the problems of society, can play a very useful role. We find that no clear-cut answers exist to several problems facing our society. People stand on all sides of the issues, whether in politics, economics, or in the social arena. In politics, we have some governments that do not represent or respond to people's real needs.

In economics, some governments fail to manage properly the money entrusted to them by the people. Depending on whom you talk to, governments spend too much money or too little on welfare programs for the poor. Many rich people feel that the government steals their hard-earned money from them, and hand it over to poor. They feel that the poor do not work hard enough to earn their money.

In the social arena, there are all kinds of discrimination on many different levels, such as denying people their due share because of their race, color, or gender. In the social arena, some theocratic governments impose fanatic and harmful religious practices. In an ideal world, people would elect the government that truly represents them.

It would govern effectively so that everyone in society keeps moving up on the economic and social ladder. It would provide individual freedom and ensure that every member of society is content and happy. It would energize people to accept responsibility.

We cannot find a proper balance until we learn to apply the General Universal Principle of Change to resolve these conflicts. According to this general Optimum Principle of Change, the first and the most important thing should be to select the best possible values or optimality criterion that forms the basis of the decision. Of course, constraints concerning the available resources have to be kept in mind. As stated, the problem areas lie in the details. What are the best values or the best optimality criterion, and how do we manage limited resources and other constraints to do the maximum good for society? Unfortunately, governments and people decide issues subjectively, based on their values, prejudices, and political pressures.

Proper education is the key to improving our values. The ultimate criterion should be to ensure that everyone receives the opportunity to move up the ladder. All society can and should do is to provide opportunities to every individual. Society cannot and should not attempt to redistribute wealth equally, as some socialists suggest. Such experiments with socialism and communism by several countries have failed. These countries are moving away from such attempts, since incentives are essential for individuals to do their best.

In short, a country, government, or society should strive to have good governance in terms of law and order; it should not attempt to micro-manage the economy. It should provide equal opportunities for all members of society. In the political arena, it should reflect the will of the people who should all have the opportunity to receive a proper education.

- Our Actions & General Universal Principle

What factors govern human behavior? How does an individual decide a course of action for a given situation? Why do two people react differently to the same situation? In the book *Stumbling on Hap-*

piness, Psychologist Daniel Gilbert says that the majority of us have no idea how to make ourselves happy. He goes on to say that the drive for happiness is one of the most instinctive and fundamental human impulses. Daniel Gilbert uses scientific research, philosophy and real-life case studies to illustrate several points. For example, he shows how our basic drive to satisfy our desires are misguided and link intrinsically to questions about human nature.

Pain or happiness is not associated with a situation but with our reaction to it. It is not the situation that makes us happy or unhappy, but our reaction to it. Essentially, happiness or pain is due to the chemicals generated by the brain in response to a situation. It is our mental model, which makes us react differently. Our values and belief systems make us behave the way we do. Every action or reaction starts with the mind. Before people act, they choose the optimum or the best course of action in their mind for a given situation. The process starts with the collection of data with the help of our physical senses. Our senses gather the data about a situation and transmit it to the brain. Each individual's brain already has stored neural patterns that represent the acquired 'values'. Based on the acquired values and interpretation of the available data, the brain helps one to choose the optimality criterion and a course of action.

The acquired values also include constraints. For example, some people are obsessed with making more money because of their acquired values. They are likely to choose an optimality criterion and a course of action that would maximize returns. However, they might also have acquired values that constrain them from robbing a bank to get rich. Other people may have acquired values, which places no such constraints. Physical limitations might also impose constraints. The optimality criterion and such constraints dictate the final choice.

Hindu's philosophy book Bhagavad-Gita states, "God neither acts on our behalf, nor decides our actions nor the fruits of our action. Every person acts according to one's values." We base our beliefs on our values. Bhagavad-Gita also states that people are what their values and beliefs are. God does not decide these for us, we do. Instead of blaming

God for our failures, we must learn to understand our shortcomings, and improve our efforts.

Most people usually justify their wrong actions and blame everything and everyone except themselves. Even terrorists, who decides to kill innocent people, takes such a decision based on their messed-up values. They think that they have taken the right decision, dictated by their values. Thus, at the end of the day everyone makes their own choices—rightly or wrongly based on the acquired values. We should learn to accept responsibility for our actions. We cannot simply blame others for our actions.

Simply put, one decides the course of action based on one's values after analyzing the data collected by the sensors. However, how does one acquire a certain set of values? Several factors come into play. These include the genetic makeup, the environment, and the severity of environmental changes we adjust to, while growing up. A religious person believing in pre-birth existence might also include actions from a previous life as additional factor. In one way or the other, all of these factors could contribute to one's values. Furthermore, most of these factors also have some randomness associated with them.

Recent studies on the brain show the existence of mirror neurons, which have a great impact on our social behavior. These studies indicate that that human brain is hardwired for empathy. The inferential evidence suggests that our social interaction or lack of it depends on the intensity of mirror neurons in our brain.

In fact, despite good intentions, one does not always achieve the intended goals for various reasons, some of which could be beyond one's control. What are the elements involved in the action-taking process? Besides a course of action, the following additional elements are involved in this process, namely, the capabilities of the 'doer', the tools one uses, the effort one makes, and the divine element referred to by science as an unforeseen element. Because of the variability of each of these five elements, one can never predict the outcome of an action accurately.

Let us illustrate it with a simple example. Suppose someone plans to drive from one city to another next morning. They might be the best driver, have the best car, choose the best route, and put in the best efforts. However, when the person wakes up in the morning, they might find snow and ice on the road, which introduces a new element. The person might put chains on the tire, and do everything to overcome this problem. However, some foolish driver might hit the person's car, preventing them from completing the journey. Was it destined that way as religion might suggest, or was it a random occurrence that changed the course of events? How does one settle this argument?

In any case, one cannot take all the steps simultaneously. The first step one takes is based on personal choice. The subsequent steps are also adjusted and optimized, based on the outcome in the face of unforeseen circumstances. Our values and the environment have major effects on such adjustments. A person is not all bad or good. Usually, one acquires both good and bad values, and stores them in the neural patterns. To improve our decisions, we should encourage the retention of good patterns and the removal of bad patterns.

How can we improve our values or reprogram our neural patterns in the brain? We can modify the acquired values continually through suitable practices. We cannot get away from what is hardwired in the DNA, unless geneticists come up with techniques to alter our DNA. However, the inner reflection and meditation can be a powerful tool to improve our neural patterns. It can help re-train or reprogram the mind and reshape our values. Parents, society, and religion can play an important role by changing the environment and providing opportunities for proper education. Unfortunately, many religions make it worse by indoctrinating children with narrow-minded beliefs and imposing their version of good and bad.

How do we decide what is good or bad? A universally acceptable definition of a bad action would be one that hurts anyone, including oneself, physically, socially, economically, or emotionally. Good, of course, is the opposite of bad. Everyone commits some good and some bad deeds because of mixed values. When a person commits a bad deed, they fail to make proper decisions because of poorly acquired values; poor access to the values, or improper analysis by the brain. Sometimes, people with predominantly good values can also exercise poor judgment and commit a crime.

A person's intentions are very important in deciding whether that person is doing a good deed or committing a crime. For example, a person intending to kill someone with a knife will be committing a crime. However, a surgeon using the same tool might operate on someone to save his or her life. The surgeon might fail to save the life and the person might die. The result is the same; death, but the difference is that the killer committed a crime and the surgeon did not.

How should society punish one who commits a crime? For its smooth functioning, society has to ensure that individuals assume responsibility for their own actions. Obviously, a person is temporarily insane when they commit an insane act like murder. However, temporary insanity should not be a defense and a person must accept responsibility for their actions and face the consequences. Society does have the responsibility to provide an environment for nurturing better values. Ideally, society should put a criminal in an environment where their values can be modified and they can be retrained and rehabilitated. Incarcerating a person and throwing them in a jail is unlikely to improve their values. Ultimately, it all comes down to our values, stored in the form of neural patterns inside our brains.

- Genes and Chemicals Affecting Behavior

Francis Collins, the scientist leading the Human Genome Project, announced that we might shortly find out more about important new gene sequences governing aspects of personality, such as intelligence and behavior. Collins also stressed that besides understanding the genes governing behavior in the Human Genome Project, the focus is also on identifying the faulty genes responsible for diseases such as diabetes, heart disease, cancer, and mental illness.

Another frontier where success would pay handsome dividends is the study of areas of the brain, known to be involved in processing dopamine. Drugs such as dopamine produced and distributed in the brain are mainly responsible for our moods and compulsive behavior such as drinking and gambling. Harvard Medical School and Mayo Clinic recently conducted studies using magnetic resonance imaging tools mapping activity in the brain area involved in dopamine processing. These studies found that certain areas lit up when gamblers gambled, just like drug and alcohol users. These areas became active when gamblers won or anticipated winning.

Our body produces chemicals like dopamine, released in the nucleus accumbens and the frontal cortex in the brain. This dopamine floods the synaptic gap between the nerve endings and binds to receptors on the adjacent cells, activating more neurons involved in memory and emotion, and thus generating a feeling of pleasure. Chemicals, such as opioids/endorphins, are also released by neurons to numb pain, or to prevent the pain signals from reaching nearby cells. This produces a feeling of pleasure or euphoria elsewhere in the brain.

Neuroscientists at the University of Michigan discovered that the amount of pain one suffers is partly due to a gene that helps regulate how many natural painkillers, endorphins, the body produces. The gene produces an enzyme called COMT that metabolizes the brain dopamine, which acts as a signal messenger between brain cells. The activity of COMT depends on which amino acid it contains. Zubieta discovered that people with two copies of the val-COMT did not feel as much pain as people with two copies of met-COMT.

Taking certain drugs can also create an artificial high. Narcotics mimic opioids, cocaine triggers the release of dopamine, and alcohol and nicotine affect both dopamine and endorphin circuits, producing a feeling of euphoria. They found that the dopamine receptors in the brain might multiply in the presence of certain drugs such as cocaine, letting more drugs enter and activate nerve cells. In addicts, the brain's inhibitory system is also weak.

Various drugs interfere with the natural trigger mechanisms for dopamine and endorphins, and repeated use can fool the brain into craving those drugs thus leading to addiction. People can alter the state of their minds through chemicals or drugs, and can get high and experience through delusion a false reality far removed from the actual reality. Most of these mind-altering drugs are harmful and highly addictive. However, research by pharmaceutical companies might discover new medicine that can correct various brain mechanisms and help cure addiction.

- Natural Selection vs. Artificial Selection

Nature has taken a long time using the Natural Selection Principle to optimize the genome sequence and adapt to the environment. It has been experimenting with different permutation combinations of the base pairs of A, C, T, and G; stretching them into a sequence of 3 billion letters that contains the entire history of human evolution. To emphasize the idea of this experimentation and critical pairing, if we just altered three particular letters out of three billion in a particular gene, it would result in the cystic fibrosis disease.

Olson also made an interesting observation in a lecture at the University of Washington. He said that the human genome has a finite sequence, although it is long and takes about 500,000 pages to print the DNA sequence composed of A, C, T, and G. He also said that once we can bind and clearly define a problem, the human brain has the frightening ability to bring any problem, irrespective of its complexity, to its knees and solve it. The solution may not be in the neat form of cause and effect because of the complexity of the problem, resulting from large number of connections and permutation combinations.

According to Olson, researchers now have a designer mouse and it is possible to have a designer human. Through artificial selection, we can deliberately impose change by tinkering with various genes as opposed to the Natural Selection process. However, we must be very careful when we try to do so. Nature has been fine-tuning the human DNA over millions of years, which has involved random experimentation in response to environmental changes and wastage of many species that could not survive. The changes imposed by researchers on the genes to achieve certain objectives, such as making a clone or certain gender, might have undesirable consequences. We cannot predict or foresee all the consequences that artificial selection, or the imposed changes on the genes, can have.

- Genetics and Religion

Returning to religion, why do we have so many different religions? How can we explain the emergence of different religions? All religions explain the reasons for their existence in their own terms. Science has attempted to explain the phenomenon of religious belief in naturalistic terms. Science also seeks answers to the following questions.

1)   Why do we find religion in almost every human group?
2)   Why do diverse cultures with little or no contact have apparent similarities among their religious views?
3)   Why do we accept non-factual statements in the name of religion?

Recent developments in the fields of neuroscience, neuropsychology, memetics, and evolutionary psychology offer the hope of finding answers to such questions and explaining religion in scientific terms. In neuroscience, work by the scientists Ramachandran and his colleagues from the University of California, San Diego, suggests evidence of brain circuitry in the temporal lobe associated with intense religious experiences. In sociology, Rodney Stark has examined the social forces that have caused religions to grow and the features that have been most successful.

For example, Stark, who claims to be an agnostic, hypothesizes that before Christianity became established as the state religion of Constantinople, it grew rapidly because it provided a practical framework within which non-family members would provide help to other people in the community in a barter system of mutual assistance. In evolutionary psychology, scientists have considered the survival advantages that religion might have given to a community of hunter-gatherers, such as unifying them within a coherent social group.

Some cognitive psychologists, however, take a completely different approach to explaining religion. Foremost among them is Pascal Boyer. His book *Religion Explained* attempts to explain religion through cognitive psychology. It lays out the basics of his theory and attempts to refute several previous explanations for the phenomenon of religion. Essentially, Boyer claims that religion is a result of the improper or over-functioning of certain subconscious intuitive mental faculties. These faculties intuitively predict physical phenomena to keep track of other people's identity, history, loyalty, etc.

As stated, the creationists have serious reservations about Darwin's Theory of Evolution. They believe that God intervened to create human beings. As if it were not enough, more controversy is on the horizon. At micro-level, we know that genes make over half a million human proteins in our body. Some of these genes also make the brain chemicals that govern our moods, thoughts, and personalities. We receive our genes from our parents, and in that sense, we exist even before our birth. Genes largely make us what we are. We do not know if souls exists or not, but if one replaces the word soul or spirit with the word gene, then we start on a long journey moving from one life to another—an idea that is proclaimed by Hinduism.

Dean Hamer, author of the book *The God Gene: How faith is hardwired in Our Genes*, claims to have discovered the God gene, which makes us more spiritual and more inclined to believe in God. Hamer makes some profound observations regarding this. He believes that every thought we think and every feeling we feel is the result of brain activity. He thinks that we follow the basic law of nature and that we are a bunch of chemical reactions running in a bag. Therefore, according to Hamer, our DNA governs the production of the brain's chemicals, which generates feelings of spirituality. Hamer claims that he has identified a gene that has codes for the production of the neurotransmitters in the brain, which regulate our mood.

Hamer came across the so-called God gene in an interesting way. While conducting a survey on smoking and addiction for the National Cancer Institute, he decided to rank over 1,000 recruits on the degree of their spiritual inclination. They used a standardized 240-question personality test, called the "Temperament and Character Inventory TCI," devised by the psychiatrist Cloninger. After ranking the participants on Cloninger's self-transcendence scale, Hamer started looking for the genes in DNA that could be responsible for the difference. Out of about 35,000 genes in human genome consisting of 3.2 billion chemical bases, he zeroed in on 9 specific genes. These 9 genes are important for the production of monoamines that regulate mood and motor control, etc. These brain chemicals include dopamine, serotonin, and orepinephrine, and the antidepressants manipulate these chemicals.

Hamer quickly discovered that a minor variation in the VMAT2 gene (for the vesicular monoamine transporter) is directly related to the scores on the self-transcendence test. Amazingly, a single change in a single base in the middle of the gene accounted for most of the difference. Hamer concluded from this observation that this gene affected spirituality, and named it the God gene. However, he points out that it does not mean that this feeling directly translates into a belief in God. Though Hamer searches for the origin of spirituality through genes, he is agnostic on the existence of God.

Hamer's efforts are part of the constant efforts of humanity to find the roots of faith. In 1979, a study completed at the University of Minnesota on over 50 pairs of identical twins yielded intriguing results. The identical twins rated similarly on the spirituality scale, but they differed in regards to their practice of an organized religion. The study seems to indicate that spirituality might be hardwired into our genes. Our environment and culture dictate the practice of organized religion. Scientists have also pushed the boundaries and investigated the effect of spirituality on the brain.

The neurologist, Newberg, from the School of Medicine in Pennsylvania University, discovered, using several imaging techniques that the deeper we delve into spirituality, meditation, or prayers, the more active the frontal lobe and the limbic system in the brain becomes. The parietal lobe at the back of the brain, orienting us in time and space, becomes dim, removing the boundaries of self and creating the feeling of being one with the universe. The increased activity in the front lobe and limbic system, combined with decreased activity in parietal lobe, can create an intense religious experience. Thus, scientists like Michael Persinger say that God is an artifact or a creation of the brain.

Of course, most religious scholars have difficulty accepting such an argument since it goes against their personal religious convictions. They believe that faith cannot be simplified down to the level of just genetic survival. Obviously, existence of the so-called God gene would separate spirituality from God, as it connects such feelings to chemicals generated by the DNA genes. However, some religions such as Hinduism, Buddhism, and Jainism, perhaps, might find the concept of gene-based spirituality interesting. Hinduism and Jainism believe in reincarnation and accept that we inherit spirituality from a previous life. In other words, the God gene, combined with genes from the DNA of our parents, could shape our physical and spiritual life.

The very fact that the concept of God appears in all human cultures seems to indicate that the concept is somehow coded in our DNA. It seems that the concept of God resides in our mind and not in other parts of our body. Right from the time man appeared on this planet, perhaps, the fear of hunger, wild animals, sickness, death, and the sense of helplessness ingrained in us a belief in a higher authority—God. The idea was coded in our genome during evolution because it was an essential element of survival. Belief in God and the emerging religions served as the mortar that held various groups together. Religion has provided order and structure for humanity. However, as stated earlier, misguided, blind, and fanatic belief in some religions has caused great misery and bloodshed for humanity.

Ursula Goodenough, a well-respected biologist who wrote a book on genetics, has recently expanded her interests from pure science to the intersection of science and religion, and has written the book, *The Sacred Depth of Nature*. She is the founder of a religious/philosophical outlook that has been called religious naturalism. She describes religious naturalism as religious responses to our understanding of nature. According to her, naturalism means knowing and understanding how nature works, how we got here, what happened, and what the universe is like.

Scientific inquiry can provide some answers to such questions. Naturalism looks at the human as a part of the whole essence of nature, and thus she includes in naturalism human culture, art, philosophy, and the religious traditions of the world. In fact, Hindus worship nature in all its forms and believe that God permeates and resides in it.

4.3   *The Top Ten Mysteries of Life*

Several questions concerning life and its meaning remain unanswered, especially from the religious pint of view. The top ten questions that need to be answered in a satisfactory manner are therefore listed below. We shall return to the discussion of these mysteries in the final chapter.

1) If a DNA molecule is the source of human life, how did it achieve its present form?

2) If all parts of the human body are interdependent, interrelated, and interconnected, forming a complex adaptive system, how does such a complex adaptive system develop, starting with a single cell in the womb?

3) If genes make proteins, enzymes and all the chemicals that govern our growth, moods, thoughts, behavior and personalities, how did different genes evolve, and how does a particular gene become active for a particular cell?

4) If some particular gene prolongs the life span (seems reasonable to assume when we look at certain families), can we manipulate it to prolong life and its quality?

5) If the brain is the master controller that projects our personality and is responsible for our actions, how was it formed, and how does it decide what action is best.

6) Does our form of life also exist elsewhere in the universe?

7) Was there Intelligent Design for our form of life, or did it just happen to evolve?

8) Does soul exist?

9) What happens after death and before birth?

10) Does God exist, and if so how are the body, mind, and soul related to God?

Chapter 5
Science vs. Religion & Future of Life

5.1 Introduction

By now, we realize that both science and religion are far from discovering the ultimate truth about life. We simply do not have definitive answers to many basic questions concerning life such as its meaning, beginning, evolution, soul, God, and afterlife. Some say that there is no definitive, ultimate truth. We can only find our own version of truth, depending on our efforts and perception of reality. We realize that even right and wrong, like truth, are merely expressions of perception.

People unwilling to look at different perspectives are afraid of change. They justify this fear by preaching and finding faults with those who do not agree with them. They put down others, thereby, reinforcing their own self-righteous perceptions, leading to separation and hostility. Change requires taking risks and going outside of our comfort zone. Unfortunately, people afraid of taking risks never achieve much in life.

Stepping into the domain of truth requires courage as we move into unfamiliar territory. However, overcoming the fear of stepping into the unknown is the only way to find the truth. We only learn to see different points of views and develop the ability to see reality, when we let go of our set beliefs and open our mind to new ideas. In search of the truth, therefore, we must leave our comfort zone and explore new grounds.

5.2 *Science vs. Religion*

We have defined science as a set of rules or physical laws of nature (origin unknown)—an independently verifiable objective truth which attempts to explain different phenomena in terms of the causal connections in the interdependent and connected material universe.

Similarly, we can define religion as a system of subjective beliefs, which attempt to explain various phenomena. The subjective explanation differs from religion to religion. Some religions also claim that spiritual science is as exact as physical science. They claim that one can independently verify the subjective truths, but that different mental tools are required for verification.

The ultimate basis for both science and religion is the principle of causality. This principle states that every phenomenon has to have a cause, which precedes the effect. Religion believes in the Creator who is the ultimate cause of all that happens in this universe. According to them, however, causality does not apply to God, but it begins with God.

Science also believes in the cause for every phenomenon. Science has been able to discover the cause and the governing laws for many phenomena which religion attributed to the act of God. However, science has not yet found the cause for every phenomenon. For example, scientists do not know what caused the Big Bang, which is responsible for the origin of the universe. Whenever science cannot find a cause, religion interjects with the statement that God caused it.

All scientific knowledge stands on the perception of certain facts and laws on which we build our reasoning. However, such a perception of verifiable facts and reasoning for religion, similar to science, is not possible. Nevertheless, spiritual science states that in religion, unlike science where one looks outwards, you have to look inwards and analyze one's own soul to realize God. Spiritual scientists claim that that there are certain religious facts just as with science which one has to perceive, and build religion upon these perceived facts.

Spiritualists say that most people who attack religion have never looked inwards and analyzed their mind and soul. Thus, they are like blind people who deny the existence of the sun. Religion, according to them, is not in churches, mosques, or temples; it is just a perception. The only real religious people are those who have truly perceived God and the soul. Nevertheless, one can never prove or disprove the existence of God by argument.

Science tells us that the origin of life in this universe was the result of random permutations and combinations of chemical molecules. Science further claims that such random experimentation was the key element in the process of the evolution of life, which was driven by the Natural Selection principle. This principle let all species compete for survival in the dynamically changing environment and navigate the associated constraints. . Many species, which cannot compete, simply perish in the process. The ones that survive continue to prosper and evolve. Science thus believes in the Theory of Evolution and not creation or Intelligent Design.

Science essentially describes a living entity as a sophisticated mechanism put together by human DNA. According to science, a human body is just an assembly of several mechanisms put together by the DNA code. All emotions, feelings, and actions originate in the brain because of interaction with the outside world through the body sensors. In fact, the actions directed by our mind; based on the processed data according to the acquired patterns, define our personality. Such actions by the mind generate different chemicals, which dictate our mood and feelings of pain and pleasure. The so-called conscience or awareness is thus the result of the projection of a person's individuality by the mind. Science does not directly support the notion of soul.

Religion, on the other hand, claims that random experimentation simply cannot lead to the evolution of human life of such incredible complexity. Furthermore, it believes that any form of life cannot evolve from lifeless chemical elements. It advances the theory of creation or Intelligent Design in place of the Theory of Evolution. These theories suggest that there was a pre-planned Intelligent Design for human life and God created human life, gave it soul and a purpose. Religion further proclaims that the Creator of human life and the incredible, complex universe is beyond our understanding. We cannot understand God or the notion of soul with our mental logic, based on sensory data. We can experience God through our soul only if we go and reach beyond the body's senses, mind, and intellect.

How do we resolve these issues or sort out the truth? With the success of science in explaining various phenomena observed in nature, and proposing theories concerning the origin and evolution of the universe and life, religion has tried to go beyond faith. Some people have attempted to find evidence to support their beliefs in creation, the Creator, soul, and life after death. Books, articles, and research theses have been written on extra-sensory perception (ESP), telepathy, clairvoyance, psi, out of body experience (OOBE), near-death experience (NDE), and reincarnation, with endless speculation on what happens after death. Authors include social scientists, such as Hans J. Eysenck and parapsychologists, such as Carl Sargent, Alan Gauld, and Stevenson, etc.

It has also been suggested that we cannot separate our own existence from that of the world outside. We are intimately associated not only with Earth, but also with the farthest reaches of the cosmos. Thus, human consciousness and the physical world cannot be regarded as distinct and separate entities. What we call physical reality—the external world—is shaped to some extent by our thoughts.

Deepak Chopra attempted to demonstrate at Stanford University that conscious mental activity exerts measurable effects on the physical world; a world that includes human bodies, organs, tissues, and cells. The mind exerts influence on our health and sickness. According to these claims, the dividing line between life and non-life is illusory and arbitrary. According to Hindu scriptures, no division, even in consciousness, is admissible at any time and the individuality of the conscience is false.

The growing interest in euthanasia, the hospice movement, experiments of Stanislav Grof with hallucinogens and terminally ill people, and research on survival reflects the trend in survival and the continuity of life. Obviously, physical existence after death is inconceivable. Since our personality is irretrievably bound up with the notion of a physical continuity, some philosophers claim that any form of survival is inconceivable.. According to Eysenck and Sargent, we shall all experience death alone and we will not know for sure whether we survive physical death until after our brain stops functioning.

Religious proponents and parapsychologists state that it would be impossible to use methods of scientific inquiry to prove religious beliefs. In this context, they point out the fact that even science has difficulty proving conclusively all the theories about the origin and evolution of universe and life. For example, they point to the knowledge gaps in the Theory of Evolution and lack of experimental verification in some the modern theories, such as string theory. Scientists need to develop reliable theories and conduct experiments using the sub-Planck scale for space and time to verify the theories of origin and the fundamental constitution of the universe. Science also has difficulty explaining the true nature and origin of space, time, and energy. Scientific models based on causality cannot take us all the way to the beginning, and explain the cause of beginning itself.

On the other hand, scientists say that just because science cannot yet explain everything or answer all the questions, one need not take refuge in religious speculations based on mere belief. They admit that there are gaps in the evolution theory. However, we should not hastily jump to the conclusion that God created all the species and human body with all its complexity, all at once, at some point in history. We must at least unveil the process and the sequential steps required for the creation of the human body, which go beyond the stories advanced by religion.

Scientists are busy addressing many of the unanswered questions regarding the present theories of origin and evolution of the universe and life. It is quite common in science to replace the existing theories with new ones. For example, Relativity replaced the Newton theory of gravitation and the Standard Model replaced the old atomic model as science discovered new facts. Many scientists refuse to accept string theory until there is at least indirect experimental verification.

- Conflict between Religion & Science

Conflict arose between religion and science as soon as they were born. They follow the opposite approaches in terms of understanding the universe and life within it. Science attempts to understand the universe and life by considering their contents and studying each phenomenon objectively. It puts together the pieces following a systematic process. Religion holds the opposite point of view and postulates that God created everything. It approaches the universe and life subjectively through proclamations from the prophets about the word of God.

For example, Hinduism claims that God is beyond time, space, and causality, and so is the soul. Man, bound by these constraints and limited in his intelligence, is incapable of understanding the true nature of the universe or life in it. It says that the reality we sense through our limited senses in time and space is just an illusion ('Maya') and not the absolute reality. The absolute reality and God can only be experienced through meditation, when we clear our mind of all thoughts. Skeptics call such a state of mind a state of delusion, since the mind can dream and visualize anything.

Religion, seeking the subjective truth, is based on faith and belief. It usually consists of different sets of unproven theories according to science. However, science is based on observations and measurable data seeking the objective truth. Any scientific theory that cannot be proved is thrown out. A religious person, believing in a theory based on their belief and faith, asks others to believe in it. Others, believing in their specific theories based on their specific belief and faith, refuse to do so. Because of such theories based on the beliefs of individuals, we find different religions often quarreling with one another.

For example, all religions believe in God but as soon as someone calls God by a different name; Ishwar, Allah, etc., people become emotional and start fighting over the name. Strangely enough, they have no problem calling water by different names in different languages. As the conflict continues between science and amongst different religions, humanity is divided into different categories. Theists and deists choose to believe in some God; atheists choose not to believe, and agnostics choose to neither believe nor disbelieve.

Scientists, of course, are always seeking more data to discover the laws of nature, which establish the cause-effect relationship for every phenomenon. Science thus expands our circle of scientific understanding as scientists find scientific answers to questions about life and our universe. Science can answer questions such as, why the sky is blue or why does it rain and many more, but it cannot yet answer all the questions. Since science does not have all the answers, religion steps in. Even when science succeeds in finding the physical laws to answer some remaining questions, religion claims that nature follows such physical laws because God wants it that way.

When the number of factors affecting a complex phenomenon (e.g. weather) is too large or randomly varying, the scientific methods fail to predict accurately. At this point, religion steps in claiming that God interferes with and alters such events. Science cannot refute this claim as religion takes refuge in subjective domains, whereas science has not yet stepped in. Nature keeps on doing its thing and does not care whether we understand its rules or laws. According to scientists, the exact prediction fails not because of the fault of nature but because we do not know all the factors or causal components. In other words, most scientists believe that it is our grasp of the profound causal connections that is lacking and not the scientific order.

The endless debate continues between religion and science. Neither side can prove or disprove the existence of God. Scientists themselves do not agree on whether God exists or not. The conflict between science and religion remains unresolved. On one side, religions keep repeating the simple answer that God created everything, including all the physical laws. However, they claim that God is beyond human intellect, and He is not bound by the usual constraints of space, time, and causality. Such assumptions close the door on any scientific discussion.

Scientists continuously defend against the onslaught of religious followers. Recently, Intelligent Design proponents are claiming that scientific understanding and physical laws just reflect the will of God. Religion keeps claiming that nature behaves in a certain way because God wants it that way.

However, science wants to learn at least what God wants. Scientists find it hard to believe different religious stories about the creation. They question the hand of some supreme authority in controlling every physical phenomenon and our daily life. Instead, they search for the physical laws that govern every phenomenon without needing direct intervention by God. The instruments and tools that scientists use to observe and process the data can be viewed as windows into the mind of God. Einstein tried to look into the mind of God to find a unified theory, but he failed.

Einstein said that science without religion is lame, and religion without science is blind. However, his notion of religion is not based on fear of life or death, or blind faith, but on striving for rational knowledge and the search for the absolute truth concerning the universe and life. According to Einstein, a scientific understanding helps to attain a humble attitude of mind, which is religious in the highest sense of the word. On the other hand, a religious doctrine, which is able to maintain itself not in a clear light but only in the dark, will lose its effect on mankind with incalculable harm to human progress.

5.3 *Science, Religion, Origin & Evolution of Life*

Let us start this discussion by asking a few questions. Can a body be just an assembly of various organs like various parts of a car or a robot? A car needs a source of energy, e.g. gasoline, and a driver. So does a body. However, unlike a body, someone needs to fill the car with gasoline and then drive it. One might think of a car with a built-in mechanism that keeps track of the amount of gasoline. When it falls below a certain level, this built-in control system, through a series of actions, could direct it to an automated gas station where it fills itself.

One might even install a computer that could possibly drive it through traffic. Nevertheless, it would need instructions from someone concerning the destination. One might even consider self-programming and learning mechanisms that could develop instructions, based on information received by sensors and/or stored patterns, and provide final directions concerning the destination.

Can a body be just like a robot and simply replenish its energy? We can build quite a sophisticated robot using computer chips, automatic feedback, adaptive control systems, and actuators, which can mimic most of the actions of a human body. Its computer can function as its brain, analyzing observed data from the sensors and reacting to it. In this computer, one could also conceivably store patterns mimicking the values stored in our brain, which form the basis of our decisions.

In other words, one can create a virtual human. Suppose such a computer inside a robot could also be equipped with self-repairing, learning and self or adaptive programming capabilities in order to make the best decision, based on certain optimality criterion in a changing environment. Would such a robot be different from a human body, except for the following facts: that man created it and not "God", it is not as complex as our body system, and it does not use biological components?

Religion claims that everybody has this life force or a conscious field, which is called a soul. Religion also claims that the human body was directly created by God, just as a watch, a car or a robot is created by a human being. Science, on the other hand, claims that the human body evolved because of evolution based on the principle of natural selection. Furthermore, we know that a human body can sustain itself with the help of sophisticated built-in control systems. Such built-in body mechanisms can seek energy sources, then convert and utilize this energy to sustain and grow the body.

However, the human body, as religion claims, would also need a life force or some sort of self-programming capability to guide its journey through life. Science has failed to detect any such singular configuration of a conscious field, life force, or soul. It cannot prove the existence of a conscious field permeating everybody. Nevertheless, science does accept terms such as consciousness or one's personality projected by the mind, based on the integration of the data sensed by the physical senses.

Is human life more significant, and does it have a purpose? We human beings obviously think so, mainly because of our ego and our thinking that human life is special and different from other forms of life. However, there are some people, who think that there is no difference between that of a human life and an ant's life in this vast universe except for different body structures, as both appear and disappear with different life spans and the universe hardly takes notice. According to them, we exist but there is no real purpose or meaning of life.

Then, there are those who think that human life is superior to the other forms of life because of our intelligence, and that life has a meaning and purpose. They point out that only the human mind is capable of understanding this universe and life in it. Finally, there are those, mostly religious people, who think that God specially designed us for a specific purpose. They think that we were chosen by God to rule over the animal kingdom and this world.

How should we react to these points of view? We must keep an open mind, because all of them are attempting to seek the ultimate truth. It seems that when science discovers all the answers and religion or spirituality is properly understood, they might converge on the same truth. Genetic science is showing the way. It has already shown that the human brain, composed of neuron cells (or DNA with certain genes activated), controls and guides our destiny and emotions.

Genetic science has also shown that every individual's DNA is distinct and it is affected by the environment and our behavior or lifestyle. We also know that genetic information from a parent's DNA is directly passed onto their newborn baby, forming the basis of their baby's DNA.

Almost all religions discuss the notion of soul and God, and the relationship between the two. Earlier, we presented a very fascinating

Hindu point of view relating to the soul and God. It claimed that the soul and God are the same (fields), and the soul is just a reflection of God. We illustrated this concept of Advaita or 'not two but one' with the help of two analogies. The first analogy was that various pots, filled with the same air, are polluted just as an individual's soul is polluted and bonded.

The second analogy was of the sun (God) reflected from different water-filled pots (souls). Yet another way to explain the concept would be to think of the same electromagnetic field inside each house, which plays the same music video on a TV when tuned to the same station. The quality of the picture depends on the communication channel, antenna, and the TV set.

Science might not accept the religious concept of soul, suffering, and the search for potential divinity. However, science as well as religion is interested in the top ten mysteries of life, and both understand the importance of resolving these mysteries.

To summarize these top ten mysteries; both science and religion accept that the DNA molecule leads to human life, although religion does not accept it as a direct and ultimate source of human life. Both accept that parts of our body are interdependent, interrelated, and interconnected; forming a complex system. Both understand the importance of genes in making proteins, enzymes, and all the chemicals that govern our growth, moods, thoughts, behavior, and personalities. Both accept that our brain is the master controller—although religion goes beyond the notion of mind to soul to the ultimate master, God. Both are curious to find out if our form of life exists elsewhere and both accept the importance of intelligence in our life.

However, religion accepts Intelligent Design for our form of life, but science accepts evolution through the principle of natural selection. Religion believes in the existence of the soul and God based on faith, but science needs proof. Science does not accept the concept of soul. Science develops a link between the body, mind, and intelligence; but religion goes further and links them to the soul and to God.

We notice that neither science nor religion have all the answers, though people of strong faith believe they do have all the answers. Nevertheless, it should not be difficult for science and religion to agree on certain things as the search goes on for all the answers. For example, they can agree that it is our responsibility to strive to improve our values or our DNA for the sake of future generations.

We all accept the continuous modification of our individual DNA molecule in various life cycles. We also know that a parent's traits are passed on to their child's DNA, although we do not know for sure what aspects of the cultural evolution are also passed on. Could it be that a DNA molecule might finally reach a stage which science might call perfection, and meet the religious realization of potential divinity or merger with God?

Let us summarize what we have observed during our journey thus far regarding the role of science and religion in understanding the origin and evolution of life

Science—Origin & Evolution of Life

Life has two basic characteristics: A living being must sustain and reproduce itself. In other words, it must have a set of instructions and a mechanism to carry out these instructions to sustain and reproduce. These biological mechanisms in normal living beings are the metabolism and genes. The normal cycle for a living entity (including plants) includes birth, growth, reproduction, decay, death, and the continuation of the species through its seeds. Life on earth is based on chains of carbon and a few other atoms, such as nitrogen or phosphorous. Appearance of Carbon item was nothing short of a miracle. As stated by Rees, six constants are required fine-tuning. Change the value of any of these constants and the nucleus of the carbon atom becomes unstable and/or the electrons collapse in on the nucleus.

How did life begin and evolve to its present form? Once again, the following picture emerges from scientific studies. According to the Big Bang model, there were no elements let alone carbon when the universe began around 14 billion years ago. It took over 9 billion years for the elements and suitable conditions to develop and thus form our solar system, i.e. about 5 billion years ago. The Earth was formed largely out of the heavier elements, including carbon and oxygen. The environment on Earth kept changing over billions of years, leading to the formation of increasingly complex organic molecules.

As this apparently random experimentation went on in the face of an ever-changing environment, catalysts in the form of enzymes were formed. Certain molecules, because of the catalytic activity of enzymes, started to reproduce themselves. Some of these molecules came to be arranged in the form of molecules of DNA. The reproduced molecules also kept changing in the random experimentation and replicating through catalytic activity. The fittest few survived but the majority that could not adapt to the changing environment simply perished. This became a continuous occurrence during what we call the process of genetic evolution.

At present, we do not know how DNA molecules first appeared. The probability of a DNA molecule forming because of random experimentation is extremely small. However, when one considers the large size of the universe with billions and billions of stars, the DNA molecules could form, despite low probability, in a few widely separated stellar systems.

One way to explain the appearance of DNA and human life on Earth would be through the application of the Anthropic Principle. In the weak form of this principle, since we happen to exist we can ask such questions as to why and how life happened on Earth. If conditions were different and led to some other form of life not based on carbon, we would be asking different questions instead.

Could the DNA on Earth have originated from some other stellar system? The answer most probably is no, because it would not survive the radiation in space. Moreover, carbon in the stars was formed less than 9 billion years ago. However, the idea that comets and meteorites seeded an early Earth with the tools to make life has gained momentum from recent observations. Scientists have recently observed some of the building blocks of life floating throughout the cosmos. For example, scientists scanning a galaxy 12 million light-years away with NASA's Spitzer Space Telescope detected copious amounts of nitrogen-containing polycyclic aromatic hydrocarbons (PAH), which are molecules critical to all known forms of life.

Continuing with the evolution of life on Earth, random experimentation appears to be the basic element of biology and is at the heart of evolution. The goal of biology becomes the replication and propagation of certain molecules that have learnt to adapt and survive. Evolution of different forms of life continues, as different DNA molecules are formed during this random process. There is a lot of wasted effort because of the inherent random nature of the change process, and the selection process is very choosy. Several forms of life corresponding to various DNA molecules originating in the process simply perish, since they cannot survive in the prevailing environment.

Nature, though wasteful, becomes efficient at the cost of being inexact. During this random experimentation process driven by the Universal Principle of Change, several genes in a DNA molecule, responsible for producing different proteins, become dysfunctional over time if they are not needed or utilized in the changing environment. A typical example would be hundreds of genes related to the sense of smell in humans, most of which are now dysfunctional.

As stated previously, the process of genetic evolution is slow since it has taken 2.5 billion years to evolve from the earliest cells to multi-cell animals. It subsequently took another billion years to evolve, through fish and reptiles, and become mammals. Genetic evolution followed the Universal Principle of Change, which involved the least effort in the process of change. This history of genetic evolution is written in a DNA molecule. The human DNA contains about three billion base pairs. Because of redundancy or inactivity, the total amount of useful information in the DNA would probably be a few million bits. One binary bit of information in an active base pair is the presence of 0 or 1 or the answer to a yes or no question.

Strangely enough, evolution picked up speed, as it took only about a hundred million years to develop from the early mammals to human beings. This was perhaps because fish contain essentially all the important components for all mammals, and it only required minor genetic changes. Genetic evolution from apes to humans probably took a few million years. The useful information in our DNA probably changed by only a few million bits during this period. Thus, the human species evolved from apes literally bit-by-bit every year (about 1 bit per year), until it learned to store and process information.

The evolution of human beings picked up another essential element that accelerated the pace of evolution. This essential element was the development of language and written information that could be passed on to future generations by means other than the genetic DNA. The cultural evolution, based on this essential element, was far more rapid than the genetic evolution based on the development of DNA.

Human DNA has not changed much during the past 40,000 years, but the pace of evolution has been phenomenal through the processing and passing of information from generation to generation. A standard book contains two million bits of information and there are more than 50,000 new books published each year in the English language alone. These books might contain useful information of the order of billions of bits at least. Thus, the information passed from one generation to another in the written form alone far exceeds the information contained in DNA.

Cultural evolution is essentially related to the capability of our brain to process information and then taking intelligent decisions. Such intelligent decisions are based on information processing by the brain using an optimality criterion and constraints, defined by an individual's values. The process of deciding the optimum course of action in a given situation starts with data collection, with the help of senses, and its transmission to the brain. As stated previously, the patterns in the form of complex neural connections in our brain, store our values. These values are at the heart of the decision-making process giving us multiple choices, learning ability and intelligence.

The Optimum Universal Principle of Change is also responsible for governing changes in our behavior and daily life. Each individual's brain has stored patterns that represent one's acquired values, which are also updated continually. For each individual, these values decide the optimality criterion and constrain choices. The learning is stored in the neural connection patterns.

The intelligence comes from the interplay of such connections in the conscious or subconscious mind. Similar to the principle of natural selection in genetic evolution, a principle of cultural selection has guided our destiny in the cultural evolution. Different optimality criteria using different sets of acquired values for selection, have led to the evolution of different societies with different traits and behavior patterns pursuing different objectives.

Religion—Origin & Evolution of Life

When we talk about life in this universe, we ask, what am I? This 'I' appears to be a projection of our personality by our mind, based on the accumulation and processing of sensory data about the environment. It also leads to the question: who am I? Various religions attempt to answer such questions by talking about the soul and God. They believe that an outside intelligence or a supreme power had planned and guided human beings and other forms of life. Most religions have serious reservations about Darwin's Theory of Evolution. Instead, they talk about Intelligent Design or the theory of creation.

The Vedanta philosophy of the Hindu religion does accept the evolution of the universe, life, and intelligence. It also introduces the concept of involution. It states the obvious fact that nothing can come out of nothing, and one cannot add any additional energy into this universe. According to the Vedanta philosophy, everything in this universe including life and intelligence originates somewhere.

The Hindu scripture Bhagavad-Gita also states that the supreme power with infinite intelligence—God—starts the cycle of creation with the laws of nature, nurtures it, and after evolution, dissolves it. The cycle continues. Thus, the universe, life, and intelligence arise from the fine form after a period of un-manifested action (involution), evolve into gross manifestations, and finally go back to the fine form.

A simple example would be a tree manifesting into a gross form from its seed after a period of inactivity, and then reverting to the seed. This cycle of evolution maintains continuous repetition for the universe, life, and intelligence ad infinitum. Thus, effect is the same as the cause, and the effect is a reproduction of the cause in a different form.

- Creation Point of View

The creationists' point of view, also disguised as Scientific Creation or Intelligent Design, is primarily based on belief. Creation theories essentially claim that God created different forms of life (e.g. fish, mice, dogs etc.) at the same time with all their parts. In other words, they do not accept Darwin's Theory of Evolution based on random experimentation and natural selection.

Creationists believe that Earth is around 10,000 years old. Different versions of the so-called theory of creation exist. For example, in progressive creation, they admit certain variability in traits within the same species. Unfortunately, there is no scientific evidence to support the claims of the creationists. According to scientific definition, it is a misnomer to give it the status of a theory.

Science needs objective truths, which can be independently experienced and verified by others. However, different religions are based on sheer belief and the faith of its followers. One cannot verify subjective religious truths like the scientific objective truths. Hindus' Raj Yoga does claim that just like science, one can perceive the religious subjective truth by learning and using the proper methods for investigation. However, such tools are again subjective, providing the means to observe the internal states and analyze our own mind.

- Intelligent Design of Life

Creationists have been trying to impose their theory on others and teach it in schools as an alternative to the Theory of Evolution. The Creationists in court lost an important case in this context in 1987. However, opponents of the Theory of Evolution, promoting the Intelligent Design theory in its place, started another movement. They argue that evolution is just a theory and so is the notion of Intelligent Design. As such, both theories need to be taught in schools.

Scientists counter this claim by emphasizing that evolution theory is based on scientific proof, and it has been tested over time. Scientists feel that Intelligent Design or creation is not science, and that students in science should only be taught the best science, as we understand it. Support for the Intelligent Design theory comes from religious fundamentalists, who consider the Theory of Evolution ungodly. It also comes from financially well-supported think tanks, mainly in the United States.

What is the Intelligent Design theory? It is not defined clearly. Essentially, it is a creation theory disguised as a new theory. The Intelligent Design theory proponents essentially argue that the very order of the universe and complexity of life demonstrates the need for Intelligent Design. They further argue that only some higher outside intelligence is capable of creating such complex life structures and diverse species. They give the example of a watch. According to them, matter unassisted by humans could not arrange itself and turn into a complex mechanical system inside a watch. Nor could matter become a human eye without outside assistance.

Similarly, they argue that different life forms with various degrees of complexity could not have evolved by themselves. The outside Intelligent Agent (God) created them. Scientists point out the fallacy of their argument by restating Darwin's assertion in his book that random experimentation and the Principle of Natural Selection indeed can lead to the evolution of highly complex systems.

To support their argument, the proponents of Intelligent Design also use the recent scientific notion that the laws of physics are 'fine-tuned' for the existence of life. They argue in favor of a divine hand in the creation of life. They say that if the universe had slightly different values of its fundamental constants, it would not have produced elements such as carbon and oxygen, and other conditions necessary for life.

However, scientists state that the fine-tuning argument assumes the existence of only one form of life. They argue that many different forms of life might still be possible with different laws and constants of physics. The main requirement for such life to evolve seems to be for stars to survive long enough to produce the elements needed for life, and allow time for the complex, nonlinear systems to work. It can be shown that different combinations of randomly varying values of the physical constants can produce different universes with stars that can survive a billion years or more. Life of some kind would most likely evolve in these possible universes.

We must state that the evolution idea is based on observed facts and well-tested scientific theory. The current evolutionary theory about the origin and evolution of life implies that evolution could and did produce the complex structures. There was no Intelligent Design or preconceived plan to make a man or even a mouse. It was the result of random experimentation. Different forms of life are merely the result of the application of the Universal Principle of Change embedding the natural selection principle.

In other words, it is simply the application of the Universal Principle of Change to molecules. These molecules are randomly changing, interacting, and surviving in a randomly changing environment, replicating and evolving. It results in random changes, leading to different and increasingly complex forms of life that could not perish but survive in the changing environment.

The evolution evidence seems to point to the evolution of life based on random processes, perturbations and the Universal Principle of Change embedding natural selection. These random changes and the results of such experimentation are coded in the genetically evolving DNA for the surviving species. The information coded in the DNA is then used to control activity in our body to insure survivability. Thus, code and control are present at every stage of the evolution of life. This code and control is indeed ingenious. Imagine creating all of the different parts of a human body from a single cell in a womb! It is nothing short of a miracle.

As stated previously, the probability of creating human DNA through random experimentation is extremely small. This gives creationists the ammunition to claim that there is outside intelligence that created and is guiding human life. Creationists also bring forth the argument that no one has been able to demonstrate in a laboratory, that putting together inorganic and organic molecules and other components of a cell, would create life from matter. Unfortunately, it is not possible to duplicate nature's random experimentation over millions and millions of years leading to the evolution of complex structures and diverse species, in a laboratory.

There are some natural reasons why different human beings have different views on the origin of life. We are all conditioned one way or the other as we grow up and develop certain values. Those conditioned to believe in some form of supreme power or God find it difficult to accept evolutionary ideas that rule out the existence of such an entity. Atheists do not want to admit any role for God, and agnostics cannot make up their minds or would like to be more open-minded, wanting more data.

Starting from the current state and tracing the steps we took to get here presents us with multiple choices. Did we have a choice? If so, what made us choose one and not the other? Did the environment randomly dictate events, or did some law of nature such as the Universal Principle of Change, subject to some optimality criterion, dictate it, or was it guidance from providence? What makes one choose a particular optimality criterion and not the other? Finally, where do the laws of nature, governing the evolution of life, come from?

Suppose 'John' entered life and progressed from state 'A' to state 'B'. What made 'John' decide to land at 'B' and not 'C'? One might ask, did 'John' have a choice and could he have ended up at 'C' instead of 'B'? A religious person might argue that he was destined and driven to 'B' because God wanted John to be at 'B' and nowhere else. A non-religious person, believing in a deterministic universe based on the causality principle, might argue that John landed at 'B' because of the laws of nature (uncertain origin). 'John's' initial state 'A' and the driving forces he was exposed to, dictated he arrive at state 'B'.

Those who believe in the uncertainty principle and the randomness introduced in the process might argue that even though 'John' could have landed at 'C' he ended up landing at 'B' instead. A believer in the anthropic principle would simply say that just because 'John' happens to be at 'B' and not at 'C', he is able to ask the question: why is he at 'B'? If he had landed at 'C' instead of 'B', he would then be asking, why is he at 'C'? Such arguments are difficult to settle.

For now, we close our discussion regarding the outside intelligence responsible for the existence of the universe and life. It is indeed easy and tempting to jump to the conclusion that some outside intelligence created the physical laws, the universe, and life. Religion loves to believe it. However, religion does not have to subject itself to the scientific rigor. It does not have to explain in causal terms how it occurred. Religion claims to know who did it, but not how. It comes up with stories that do not agree with the scientific facts. Science does not accept this leap of faith that God created our universe and life at some point in time. It demands objective proof, which is lacking.

It is heartening to note that Pope Benedict, elaborating his views on evolution for the first time as Pontiff in April 2007, said that science has narrowed the way life's origins are understood and Christians should take a broader approach to the question. The Pope also said that the Darwinist Theory of Evolution is not completely provable because one cannot reproduce mutations over hundreds of thousands of years in a laboratory.

Benedict, according to his remarks published in Germany in the book *Schoepfung und Evolution* (*Creation and Evolution*), praised scientific progress, and did not endorse creationist or Intelligent Design views on the origin of life. Benedict, a former theology professor, apparently said at the closed-door seminar with his former doctoral students that science has opened up large dimensions of reason...and thus brought us new insights.

Scientists admit that the evolution theory has gaps and certain questions remain to be answered. However, that is the case for any scientific theories such as quantum mechanics and relativity, etc. Further research keeps filling these gaps. For example, a recently developed theory of punctuated equilibrium addresses the fact that species remain unchanged for a period and then start evolving. Scientific research goes on as we test the existing theories and refine them based on newly discovered facts.

Science might not even find the ultimate answer concerning the origin and existence of the laws of nature, which are responsible for the evolution of such complex life structures and species. However, it does not mean that we hastily jump to the conclusion that some outside intelligence created the universe, the life within it, and the associated laws of nature. We should not blindly replace science with religion, if we want the spirit of inquiry to prosper. Scientists keep marching towards the ultimate unified theory that will answer all of the remaining questions.

6.   *Intelligent Life on Other Planets*

The question as to whether other intelligent life forms exist on other Earth-like planets and in our observable universe is fascinating. We must remember that for intelligent life to form on Earth too many events had to come together and many hurdles had to be overcome. Furthermore, such life form faced many threats for its continued existence. Our form of life requires energy from the sun, which will burn out in a few billion years. It also requires water and carbon, plus protection from the Earth's atmosphere and magnetic field against radiation and huge meteor impacts. Evolution also needs protection from environmental disasters that could remove water and doom life.

Despite such monumental constraints, there is a distinct probability of intelligent life similar to ours existing somewhere, and certainly of some form of intelligent life on some planets considering the vast number of them. At present, science has no proof of its existence. However, the universe is vast with billions of galaxies and billions of stars within most of the galaxies. If we assume that many of these stars have planets like our sun has then there must be a significantly large number of planets in this universe.

Astronomers estimate that about half the planetary systems discovered in our galaxy so far could contain Earth-like worlds. Scientists in the UK and USA suggest that a number of planets might have liquid water and possibly life, as published in the journal *Science* in 2006. In 2009, the NASA space agency smashed a rocket and a probe into a large crater at the lunar South Pole to find water. Scientists studied the data from the instruments and found substantial quantities of water-ice and water-vapor, the equivalent of *"a dozen two-gallon buckets"* of water.

In fact, in April 2007, astronomers detected water for the first time in the atmosphere of a planet outside of our solar system. Astronomers also discovered another far away planet, OGLE-2005-BLG-390Lb, which might be similar to Earth. This planet revolves around a dim star—Gliese 581—about 20 light years away. It could possibly support a landscape similar to Earth comprising liquid oceans and drifting continents. If so, then there is a chance that it is home to life forms, perhaps even advanced life.

Some scientists are also concerned about preserving our intelligent form of life. Hawking, in an address to the Royal Society, said that life could be wiped out by a nuclear disaster or asteroid hitting our planet. He suggested that the human race must move to a star outside of our solar system to protect the future of the species. He favored 'matter/anti-matter annihilation' as a means of propulsion to reach a planet in another star, which would take about six years traveling close to the speed of light.

7.   *Impact of Environmental Changes on Life*

How endangered is our planet and our way of life due to our actions in polluting the environment? Some recent studies suggest that we must mend our ways. In 2009, Dr. Foley reported in the journal *Nature*, the results of a team study with 27 experts from around the world. The team decided to look at the Earth's safe operating space and study the potential risks that could push our planet into a state of instability. The researchers defined nine categories of risk within that space, including global warming, ocean acidification and stratospheric ozone levels. The scientists tried to quantify the risks by compiling and analyzing published work in their particular areas of expertise. Their study suggests that we have already pushed the planet too far in at least three ways.

1) Climate researchers estimate that nature will remain in balance only as long as carbon dioxide concentrations in the atmosphere remain below 350 parts per million; yet CO_2 concentrations currently measure approximately 387 parts per million.

2) Biodiversity researchers estimate that species loss is sustainable only if we lose fewer than 10 species for every million on Earth. However, species are already disappearing at a rate of 100 species per million and projected rates are 10 times higher than that.

3) We are also dangerously close to the thresholds for freshwater use, ocean acidification, and the conversion of forests and other ecosystems into farms and cities. Crossing this threshold may lead to a cycle of global catastrophic change. Nitrogen outputs from chemical fertilizers and other human activities are already threatening to damage irreparably freshwater and marine ecosystems.

According to Dr. Foley, the changes in the environment on a global scale would change this planet into something we have never witnessed in all of human history. It is not the end of the world, but it is the end of the world, as we know it. According to Foley, we think that a little damage to the environment is acceptable but at some point, the planet will just not be able to absorb it anymore, which is especially true when it is taking multiple hits at once. The specific numbers in the study remain estimates and it will start a debate, according to Steve Carpenter of the University of Wisconsin, Madison.

This study points out, nevertheless, an important issue. We must recognize that nature has hard edges, and we cannot just keep abusing the planet forever.

According to another recent study, scientists warn that more than a third of species, assessed in a major international biodiversity study, are threatened with extinction. For example, 17,291 were deemed to be at serious risk of extinction out of the 47,677 species in the IUCN Red List of Threatened Species. These species included 21% of all known mammals, 30% of amphibians, 70% of plants, and 35% of invertebrates. However, according to some scientists, these large-scale computer simulations may be overestimating the impact of climate change on biodiversity in some regions. They think that the models that analyze vast areas do not take into account local variations, such as topography and microclimates.

It is important to note that several prominent scientists do not agree with the impact of greenhouse gases such as carbon dioxide, methane, and nitrous oxide released into the atmosphere by us. Simply stated, greenhouse gas is relatively transparent to light from the sun, but it can absorb some thermal radiation from the Earth. Normally, the Earth balances the incoming solar radiation by emitting thermal radiation. However, the presence of greenhouse substances can absorb some thermal radiation, inhibit cooling, and lead to some warming.

Should we be alarmed by the prospect of global warming? According to Dr Lindzen, Professor of meteorology at M.I.T, even a doubling of CO_2 would only upset the original balance between incoming and outgoing radiation by about 2%. He strongly disagrees with the conclusions drawn by the U.N.'s Intergovernmental Panel on Climate Change (IPCC) on the adverse impact of greenhouse gases. According to him, the measurement used in the 1,000-page IPCC Report, the globally averaged temperature anomaly (GATA), is always changing. Sometimes it goes up, sometimes down, and occasionally—such as for the last dozen years or so—it does little that can be discerned.

According to a statement issued after the last IPCC Scientific Assessment, it was likely that most of the warming since 1957 (a point of anomalous cold) was due to man. This claim was based on the following weak argument. The current models used by the IPCC could not reproduce the warming from about 1978 to 1998 without some force being applied, and thus the conclusion drawn was that the only element forcing the situation was man. The argument assumes that these models adequately deal with natural internal variability, including naturally occurring cycles such El Nino, the Pacific Decadal Oscillation, and the Atlantic Multidecadal Oscillation, etc.

However, the major modeling centers acknowledged that the failure of these models to anticipate the absence of warming for the past dozen years was due to the failure of these models to account for this natural internal variability. Thus, even the basis for the weak IPCC argument for anthropogenic climate change (changes due to CO2 emission) was shown to be questionable. According to Dr Lindzen, the notion that complex climate 'catastrophes' are simply a matter of the response of a single number; GATA, to a single forcing; CO2 (or solar forcing for that matter), represents a gigantic step backwards in climate science..

Many disasters are claimed to be evidence of warming when these disasters are simply normal occurrences. Their occurrence involves complex phenomena, dependent on the confluence of many factors. According to Dr Lindzen, the normal occasional occurrences of open water in summer over the North Pole, droughts, floods, hurricanes, sea-level variations, etc., are all taken as omens and impending doom due to our sinful ways (as epitomized by our carbon footprint). All of these phenomena also depend on the confluence of multiple factors and not just CO2.

It makes sense that one single factor, such as greenhouse gas, is not entirely responsible for climate changes. Nor do we completely understand the complex interplay of various factors and their effect on climate changes. Thus, our computer models are far from perfect. Nevertheless, it is also true that climate changes do affect our planet and species. It is also true that we are contributing to climate changes to some extent because of rapid industrialization.

At present, we might not be able to quantify the effect of our contribution to polluting the environment. Not all of us might agree on when we will reach the limits where greenhouse gases or other pollution will seriously affect the planet and our way of life. However, we must all agree that we can and must reduce pollution through our efforts. It is wise to err on the side of caution. It would thus be wise to take all the steps we can to minimize our impact on the environment. We can certainly do more in this area and improve existing structures and industrial plants, such as building new versions that will conserve energy and release less greenhouse gases and other pollutants into the atmosphere. We can strike a proper balance between industrial growth and polluting the environment by developing new technology.

Let us take an optimistic view and hope that the world community will take steps to reverse or at least prevent any further deterioration of our planet. If we do not push Earth into a state of instability, new scientific and technological discoveries promise a better future for all of us.

8. *Predicting the Future of Life*

Predicting the future is always a risky business. Predictions are difficult to make and they are usually wide of the mark. With our knowledge of past trends, we can perhaps project what will happen in the near future. Nevertheless, one can never foresee sudden and significant future changes. Abrupt future outbursts of unforeseen events could rapidly change the course of life and religion. Predicting the future can be hazardous. A quick look at the following gallery of events shows how shaky this business of predicting the future can be. Who could have predicted the following events in our brief history?

1) A New World North American Continent is discovered and the United States dominates the world as an economic, political, scientific, and technological power.

2) Hitler, Fascism, and Communism are defeated as the world moves towards freedom, democracy, and capitalism.

3) Man lands on the moon and a new era of space travel commences.

4) Humanity invents weapons of mass destruction, which could annihilate civilization.

5) Religious fanaticism leads to wars and misery for humanity.

Nevertheless, there is a single common thread that runs through the history of humankind. Somehow, good always prevails over evil in the end. The planet Earth, though polluted and endangered, still exists in this vast universe. Despite unexpected surprises, people continue to make future predictions. It is always very tempting to indulge in the exercise of predicting the future.

In my personal opinion, the following developments are likely to happen sometime during this century.

1) Science will continue unfolding the mysteries of the universe, and it will still be searching for answers concerning the origin of the laws of nature. The debate with religion will continue.

2) The application of new scientific discoveries and the resulting new technology will provide new tools to make our life more comfortable and meaningful.

3) Science will unfold the mysteries surrounding the human genome and discover how the human body evolves from a single cell.

4) Genetics will identify and learn to manipulate genes that prolong human life and improve its quality.

5) We will develop more respect for nature as we begin to understand better the interdependence and diversity of life on this planet. Humanity will realize that protecting life on our planet is critical, and it will initiate steps towards protecting it.

6) The world will come together to implement laws restraining the uncontrolled exploitation of the resources

on our planet, and stop further pollution that endangers our existence.

7) The world will place more emphasis on recycling and renewable resources.

8) Religions will learn to co-exist and become more tolerant. They would come to realize that their common goal should be uplifting of the human spirit and making this world a better place to live in.

9) Religion and science will move closer and come to an amicable settlement. They will simply agree to disagree, because science will not be able to prove with its theories and measurement techniques the alternate explanation given by religion.

10) Religion will learn to accept irrefutable scientific discoveries, and science will venture out into the field of consciousness. Both will realize that they share the same common goals; namely, understanding the universe and life within it.

Chapter 6
Final Destination—The Ultimate Truth

6.1 Introduction

Do we know the ultimate truth? As we come to the end of our journey, we realize that neither science nor religion has all the answers about life. We shall address the following questions in this chapter. What is the meaning of truth? What is the ultimate truth about our life, its origin, and evolution? We have already discussed what science and religion have to say about the mysteries of life. However, let us go on with our search and discuss further some questions. Let us summarize what we know, and speculate about what we do not know yet.

6.2 The Meaning of Truth

What is the ultimate truth about life, and can we ever discover it? How do we go about searching for the ultimate truth? Einstein once said that no problem could ever be solved at the same level of consciousness that created it. In search of truth, therefore, we must leave our comfort zone and search for the truth from different perspectives. We should go in search of the truth and see how far our intellectual capabilities take us. As we search for the ultimate truth, we might find that we cannot discover it because of our intellectual limitations or due to the constraints of time, space, and causation imposed on our mind. Nevertheless, we might at least get a glimpse of it, and see some light at the end of the tunnel.

150

To find the truth, we must first understand the exact meaning of truth. Let us first examine the various elements involved in discovering truth itself. Our mind plays a critical role in deciding the truth. Some people even claim that no universal, definitive, ultimate truth exists that stands on its own. Despite one's best efforts, one can only find one's own version of truth, depending on one's perception of reality. According to Indian sage and philosopher Patanjali, proven theories derive their proof from one or the other of the following sources (also translated in the book *Patanjali's Vision of Oneness—An Interpretive Translation by Swami Venkatesananda*)

1) Direct perception, sense-experience, or intuition
2) Deduction or extension of direct perception and sense experience or beliefs
3) In the absence of direct proof or experience, indirect proof deduction from the right or wrong application of principles of logic chosen by one, often leads to vague generalizations or presumptions that since the theory comes from a usually reliable source, it must be correct.
4) Scriptural or other trustworthy testimony or authority, where one accepts as proof, the statements of those who one has accepted as the authority. Such acceptance is faith-based, blind, and fanatic.
5) Unsound thinking or wrong knowledge based on error and mistaken identity. In this case, the cognition is unreal and faulty and hence the knowledge is faulty too. There is no agreement between the expression and the experience, between the substance and the description.

Since our mind decides what we accept as the truth, we are limited by its ability to understand the meaning of truth. According to Patanjali, there are five states that our mind experiences.

1) Proven thinking assumed to have been reliably proved, and thus constitutes the right knowledge
2) Unsound thinking, wrong knowledge, false assumptions, presumptions, beliefs, deductions, or inference

3) Hallucination or imagination totally unrelated to any proven or assumed theories, including the delusion
4) A state of dullness or sleep, succumbing to the movement of thought; feeling that it is impossible to go beyond it
5) Memory or the recollection of a teaching or an experience, giving rise to the notion that it is possible to go beyond the movement of thought. Such a notion forms an image

6.3 Human Limitations

We must first understand our limitations and accept the fact that our interpretation of the reality of the universe can be flawed. When we talk about the material world or the universe, we are looking outwards from the inside of our brain. We thus want to look at the form and the structure of the entire universe. It is as if someone locked inside a bottle is trying to read the label on the outside of the bottle. Alternatively, someone locked inside a room will want to know how the room looks from the outside. Unless one can step outside, one cannot get the complete picture.

We are part of the whole, and the part wants to understand the whole. It is like a tiny part of our body trying to understand the workings of the entire body. However, some scientists believe that our universe is like a hologram. In a hologram, the entire form and the structure are enfolded within each part, and each part contains enough information to reconstitute the whole. If this premise is true, we do have a chance to understand the real universe.

The most important difference between human beings and animals is the human brain, which developed during the process of genetic evolution. It contains about one trillion cells with 100 trillion connections between those cells. Although we use less than 10% of the neuron cells, they can make very complex connections resulting in complicated patterns. Our brain is fast, large, and a highly intelligent computer, but it has limitations. It can process and interpret data only to a limited extent, observed by our limited sensors. Our intelligence is finite and it appears that the finite cannot understand the infinite. Our brain is also a prisoner of the notion of time, space, and causality.

Thus, our perception of the reality and the universe is not absolute. Our attempt to perceive the true nature of this vast universe, through the limited interpretation of the data, is like seven blind people trying to visualize an elephant. Even terms such as time, space, etc. that we define to express our understanding of the universe, need better definitions and generalization. Unless we understand how our brain formulates understanding, we cannot truly understand this universe. This understanding of the brain might not solely rely on modern science. The knowledge of modern biology may provide corroborative evidence, but it is not a pre-requisite. Perhaps we might perceive the ultimate truth only by inner reflection, intuition, and meditation, as the sages claim.

Nevertheless, even in modern science, despite the marvelous success of neuroscience throughout the past century and developments in artificial intelligence, we are far from completely understanding the cognitive processes. For example, we can quickly recognize the solution to a problem but computer can quickly verify but not recognize the solution quickly. This P vs. NP conjecture that if computer can quickly verify an answer, can it also quickly find that answer, carries a prize of $1 million for the proof. The basic difficulty lies in understanding various neuron connections, formation and identification of patterns, and the brain signal processing mechanisms. These are collectively responsible for cognitive activity and decision-making. Finally, our brain processes data and comes up with solutions and decisions based on our previously stored knowledge, values and compatible optimality criteria.

The brain cannot be modeled as a simple cause-effect model because of the large number of connections. On one hand, when we drive a car in traffic for example, our brain takes decisions based on fuzzy logic without solving all the dynamic equations. On the other hand, it is capable of understanding the most exact logic. Scientists are trying to gain a better understanding of the brain. They are also attempting to build intelligent computers with the capability to make complex connections like neurons make in our brain, and process the data intelligently. If that happens, we might be able to amplify our intelligence just as the other machines amplified our mechanical power, and get a better picture of the universe.

Since we do not know the ultimate truth about life, let us speculate and comment on the interesting feature and the top ten mysteries of life.

- Interesting Features of Life

1. Life has two basic characteristics: A living being must sustain and reproduce itself. Biological mechanisms; namely metabolism and genes implement instructions to sustain and reproduce. The normal life cycle includes birth, growth, reproduction, decay, death, and continuation of the species.

2. Life develops and continues through the DNA molecule—a schema in a single cell. The cell; an independent living entity, depends on all sorts of complex interaction within itself. It divides, transforms, and differentiates itself into new type of cells leading to a complex organism like humans.

3. All parts of the human body are interdependent, interrelated, and interconnected, forming a complex adaptive system.

4. Genes make the proteins in our bones, the enzymes that digest our food, the hormones that control our reproduction and all the chemicals that govern our growth, moods, thoughts, behavior, and personalities.

5. The human body is an incredibly complex chemical factory that produces all sorts of chemicals. In fact, the

maintenance of good health boils down to the chemical balance in the body.

6.   The brain is the master controller that projects our personality and gives meaning to life. It is part of the nervous system, which controls and integrates the activities of all parts of the body. It collects, processes, and responds to information. It can visualize but mainly process and interpret the data observed by our limited sensors to a limited extent.

7.   It is only through the processing of data by the brain that we learn about the universe and life. Furthermore, our brain generates all feelings including spirituality and faith in God.

8.   Despite the marvelous success of neuroscience throughout the past century and developments in artificial intelligence, we are far from completely understanding the cognitive processes. The basic difficulty lies in understanding dynamic neuron connections, the formation and identification of patterns, and the brain signal processing mechanisms.

9.   Science or religion does not have definitive answers to many questions concerning life, such as its true meaning, exact beginning, details of evolution, the soul, God, and the afterlife.

10. The complexity of the universe and life is awe-inspiring and overpowering. Our intelligence is simply too inadequate to understand all of the complex interactions and processes related to life.

6.4   *The Top Ten Mysteries of Life—Comments*

Let us return to the top ten mysteries of life. All of these mysteries are difficult to unfold, and at present, we do not have any definite answers. Nevertheless, we can give some plausible explanations and comments, as follows.

1) *If a DNA molecule is the source of human life, how did it achieve its present form?*

As stated in this book, science presents the following scenario for the evolution of life. Beginning with the Big Bang, it took over 9 billion years for the necessary elements and suitable conditions to develop before our solar system could form, around 4.5 billion years ago. The Earth was formed largely out of the heavier elements, including carbon and oxygen. The Earth's environment kept changing, leading to the formation of increasingly complex organic molecules.

Permutation, the combination of carbon, and other inorganic elements under varying environments, led to the formation of organic compounds. The random experimentation went on in the face of a constantly changing environment. Certain molecules, because of the catalytic activity of enzymes, started to reproduce themselves. Some of these molecules arranged in the form of molecules of DNA. The process of evolution led to the creation of a simple living cell. Such a cell could survive in the then prevailing environment. The fittest few survived but most that could not adapt to the changing environment simply perished.

DNA molecules also kept changing in the random experimentation and replicating through catalytic activity. This process led to the evolution of diverse life. Nature has taken a long time to optimize the genome sequence and adapt to the environment. Scientists have mapped the human genome. Scientists can modify the DNA molecule to some extent, however; they were not able to replicate this complex DNA—schema—in a laboratory. Scientists thus believe that life evolved from a simple cell through random experimentation and the process of natural selection.

In 2010, researchers were able to construct a bacterium's "genetic software" and transplant it into a host cell. The resulting microbe looked and behaved like the species "dictated" by the synthetic DNA. It would seem that the evolution of human DNA was not a purely random phenomenon, as the Universal Principle of Change dictated it. As human brain developed and started processing information more effectively, it became capable of taking optimum decisions. This cultural evolution thus accelerated the process of evolution.

Most religions do not accept the Theory of Evolution. They argue that only higher intelligence is capable of creating such complex life structures and diverse species. They believe in creation—that God created man and woman directly. Most religions claim that God is the Creator of our universe and life.

They claim that God is eternal, and that no one created God. Some religions believe in evolution to the extent that God first created life in a cell, and it was not a random phenomenon, as scientists believe. Once life was created, it led to the evolution of complex life on the planet under the supervision of God, giving meaning to human life.

2) *If all parts of the human body are interdependent, interrelated, and interconnected, forming a complex adaptive system, how does such a complex adaptive system develop, starting with a single cell in the womb?*

Nature, starting with the union of a male sperm and a female egg, takes about nine months to make a baby in mother's womb. At conception, a DNA molecule inside the nucleus of a cell is fused together from two sets of chromosomes, one set given by each parent. On day one, it starts with a fertilized egg. The developing embryo eventually becomes the fetus in the womb of a pregnant woman and multiplies into 100-150 cells within a week. These Embryonic Stem (ES) cells continue to multiply and begin to specialize and differentiate themselves. The embryo, known as a gastrula at this stage, contains three distinctive germ layers. The descendants of these three layers go on to form ultimately hundreds of different tissue types in the human body.

We do not have a complete understanding of the processes that take place inside a womb. Imagine creating all the different parts of human body, different cells, etc., from a single cell in a womb. It is nothing short of a miracle. A tremendous amount of signaling must happen between cells during the development process to ensure that everything ends up in the right place. Small changes in these signaling processes can have very large effects.

Scientists are investigating the effect of small changes in DNA patterns during embryonic development. Our DNA correctly creates and wires up millions of cells every minute in a developing fetus in the womb. This is a complex process through which the human genome, with several thousand genes, is able create a human body. The human body contains trillions of cells, billions of carefully wired neurons and hundreds of different cell types, forming organs as diverse as the heart and the eyes.

3)   *If genes make proteins, enzymes, and all the chemicals that govern our growth, moods, thoughts, behavior and personalities; how did different genes evolve and how does a particular gene become active for a particular cell?*

Genes are identically present in each of our cells, but they act in different combinations. They turn on and off like switches several times a second and send complex signals through chemical reactions to our cells, directing their activity.

According to Collins, the scientist leading the Human Genome Project, we will soon know important new gene sequences that govern various aspects of personality such as intelligence and behavior. In another study, scientists showed that minimal changes in an amino acid on a single gene have a profound effect on speech processing in humans. Recently, scientists synthesized a gene in a laboratory that was a precursor to an existing gene in an animal. However, we have just scratched the surface in this field. We still have a long way to go before we can answer questions regarding evolution and the proper role of different genes.

4) *If some particular gene prolongs the life span (seems reasonable to assume when we look at certain families), can we manipulate it to prolong life and its quality?*

Scientists have accelerated research on aging and prolonging the human life span. Dr. Langmore and his group at the University of Michigan have been studying human DNA molecule, the essence of human life. Specifically, they are looking at the tips of the DNA molecule, telomeres, which is part of the double-helix molecule that contains a kind of chain of repeating pairs of enzymes.

Another 2006 report in Biology Journal indicated that Resveratrol, a natural phytoalexin found in grapes and red wine, increases longevity in the short-lived invertebrates. Sinclair believes that resveratrol works by activating SIRT1, a gene that seems to play a fundamental role in controlling life span. Biologists have found that increasing the expression of SIRT1 slows aging. However, as research intensifies on aging, we might see some surprising developments.

5) *If the brain is the master controller that projects our personality and is responsible for our actions, how is it formed and how does it decide the optimum course of action?*

A few thousand genes in the human genome tell 100 billion neurons to wire themselves precisely in the human brain. The signaling mechanisms that wire up the 100 billion cells in the human brain are complex. We do not understand how so few genes can meticulously wire so many neurons. In short, we know so little about our brain—the master controller.

6) *Does our form of life exist elsewhere in the universe?*

Our form of life requires energy from the sun that will burn out in a few billion years. It also requires water and carbon, protection from the Earth's atmosphere and magnetic field against radiation and huge meteor impacts. According to the Theory of Evolution, the evolution of life also needs protection from environmental disasters that could remove water and doom life. Despite such monumental constraints, there is a distinct probability of intelligent life similar to ours, and certainly of some form of intelligent life on other planets taking into account the large number of them.

In 2008, NASA announced that scientists have detected organic molecules, methane, and water in the atmosphere of an extra solar planet known as HD 189733b. The planet is located 63 light-years away in the constellation Vulpecula. However, it is so massive and so hot that it is unlikely to be a host for any kind of life, let alone intelligent life. Nevertheless, scientists keep looking for the signs of intelligent life elsewhere in the universe. Stephan Hawking, for example, is confident that intelligent life does exist elsewhere, and it could pose a potential risk to our planet.

7) *Was there an Intelligent Design for our form of life or did it just happen to evolve?*

The Intelligent Design theory proponents essentially argue that the very order of the universe and complexity of life demonstrates the need for Intelligent Design. They further argue that only a higher outside intelligence is capable of creating such complex life structures and diverse species. They also use to support their argument, the recent scientific notion that the laws of physics are 'fine-tuned' for the existence of life. They argue in favor of a Divine hand in the creation of life. They say that if the universe had slightly different values of its fundamental constants, it would not have produced elements such as carbon, oxygen, and other conditions necessary for life. Evolutionists, of course, do not agree, and claim that complexity and intelligence can evolve from random experimentation following the Principle of Natural Selection and from cultural evolution..

8) *Does soul exist?*

Almost every religion believes in the existence of a soul inside the body—the life force that differentiates the living from the dead. It exists even after the body dies. According to most religions, the soul is considered the true master of the body. Does the soul really exist or is it a fiction of human imagination? Science has no evidence and it has not detected soul or any such field. Science, therefore, does not admit the existence of such a life force or soul. At present, the question remains unanswered for nonbelievers.

9)   *What happens after death and before birth?*

One of the reasons for belief in a religion is the human desire for some sort of continuity in the afterlife. Most religions believe in Heaven and Hell, where the soul eventually goes as a reward or punishment for one's actions. Hinduism believes in Heaven and Hell as a temporary abode for the soul. It believes in the continuity of life, as the soul moves from one body to another until it merges with the supreme soul—God. According to Hindu scriptures, the soul or conscious field carries with it the essence of a past life, on leaving the body, during death into a new body. Several cases have been reported about someone remembering a past life.

In a way, science also admits the continuity of life though not in the sense a religion does. If we plant a seed and nurture it, it leads to the growth of a tree. The tree produces more seeds, which leads to the growth of more trees. Similarly, a human DNA cell is capable of starting a life that can grow into a human body and propagate life before the body dies. The DNA carries forward quite a few traits of the parents into the next body. However, religion talks about the soul and not the human DNA.

According to religion, since energy cannot be destroyed, the soul never dies. On death, this energy (soul field) leaves the body. Hindus believe that the soul (a singular configuration of energy) carries with it the sum total of our existence. This field (soul) might enter another body and continue its journey. The journey ends when this field (soul) becomes free from the extraneous field carrying the past memory field. The soul is thus liberated from bondage, and the field leaving the body merges with the entire energy field, or becomes one with God.

10)   *Does God exist and if so how are body, mind, intelligence, and soul related to God?*

Religion believes in God or the Creator, known by different names, who is responsible for the creation of the universe and life within it. Different religions attribute different qualities to God. However, most of them agree that He is benevolent, kind, and loving. Several scientists believe that Hinduism come close to science as far as the concept of God is concerned.

Hinduism claims that God is a super-conscious field endowed with infinite intelligence that can manifest in many forms. God is the energy field that permeates the entire universe. God is the cause of everything. God creates the universe and life and all the laws of nature, but God is beyond space, time, causality, and the ensuing laws of nature.

However, nonbelievers have a problem when one associates consciousness or intelligence with this description of God as an energy field. We know that we do have energy fields such as electromagnetic waves that contain data, information, and knowledge. The fields surrounding us contain all kinds of information and we need a proper antenna and receiver to extract this information. However, most scientists have problems accepting the existence of intelligent or conscious fields, which can change, defy, or even affect the normal outcome of an expected event according to the laws of physics.

Most religions agree that there is an intimate personal relationship between God and the soul. Just as atoms are the constituents of matter, the souls (conscious fields) are parts of God (the super-conscious field) according to Hindu scriptures. Bhagavad-Gita, a Hindu scripture says that God, the supreme conscious energy field, neither likes nor dislikes any soul or sub-field. He neither punishes nor favors anyone. We punish or reward ourselves through our actions. We are responsible for our own actions and we must face the consequences of our actions. According to Hindu's Theory of Karma, what we did in the past decides our present, and what we do now decides our future.

Actions are taken based on individual values stored in one's brain, which are continually modified by such actions. We must constantly strive to improve our values. However, the Hindu scripture Bhagavad-Gita, also says that the outcome of any action depends on five elements: motivation, a 'doer' mentality, tools, effort, and the surrounding environment. In this sense, God, the surrounding field, does affect the outcome.

People usually worship and pray to God asking for favors. Does God respond to prayers? Most religions believe in the power of prayers. God would most probably not directly interfere or change the outcome of an action. If He did, it would be hard to grant contradictory prayers; for example, a farmer asking for rain and the potter not wanting rain.

A more appropriate question that we must ask is, can prayers help strengthen our 'values'? If we think correctly, then our decision is more likely to produce the desired result. We are likely to use proper tools, the right type of effort, and act when the environment or the surrounding field is more favorable. Meditation, or praying to God to inspire our mind and channel our energy in the right direction, could strengthen our values and resolve. The best favor one could ask for is the intelligence to make good decisions. For example, the most important prayer in the spiritual philosophy of Hinduism, Gayatri mantra, is to ask God for the enlightenment of the mind.

Finally, what is intelligence and how did we acquire it? We do not have a satisfactory answer to this question. According to Swami Vivekananda, a Hindu philosopher, God means universal intelligence. This infinite cosmic intelligence, always present, firstly becomes involved, manifests itself, evolves, and becomes perfect again. The cycle thus continues ad infinitum. Intelligence is what makes us human and the goal of human life is to keep evolving until it achieves supreme intelligence, which starts the next cycle.

Hindu Upanishad describes the relationship between the body, mind, intelligence, and soul as follows. It compares the soul as the master of a chariot, and the body as the chariot. The brain, the seat of intelligence, is compared to the driver of the chariot (the body). The body's senses are compared to the horses pulling the chariot (the body), grazing in this external world (field), with the mind compared to the reins on the horses (senses).

The goal of life is to train and keep the horses (senses) in check through the reins (the mind) by the driver (the brain), so that the soul (the master) can reach its destination and merge with the supreme soul—God. Usually, poor decisions by the driver (the brain) lead to loosened reins (the mind), which lets the horses (senses) run wild, taking the soul for a ride and preventing it from reaching its destination. In view of such actions, the master (the soul) bound to nature, stays on an almost endless journey.

6.5 Science & Religion—Final Words

To summarize, science and religion were born, as shown in Fig. 6.1

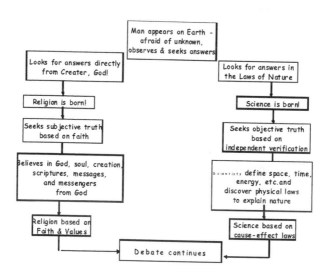

Fig 6.1—Birth of Science & Religion

Human appears on Earth, observes various phenomena, and struggles to survive in the hostile environment. As humans try to explain everything happening around them including their own existence, they take two different approaches. Scientists move on a path that shows that life evolves due to certain causal laws and random experimentation, whereas religious people put their faith in a divine act.

- Random Vs. Divine

There is a concurrent theme running through all discussions concerning the origin and evolution of life. Science attributes origin and evolution to causal laws of nature and random processes, whereas religion attributes them to divine acts. Science claims that there was a Big Bang, which was responsible for the origin of the universe. Furthermore, the universe and life evolved mainly in accordance with the laws of nature, whose origin is uncertain.

Science introduces an element of uncertainty through quantum mechanics, which makes the outcome non-deterministic. Quantum mechanics claims that there are so many possible outcomes for any event, but an observer observes only one. Can an observer change an outcome because of the element of uncertainty introduced by quantum mechanics? Few believe that we can remove the element of uncertainty and change the outcome.

Religion, on the other hand, claims the supreme power—God created the universe and life within it. The creation and evolution of the universe and life, and the events that we observe in nature are according to His will. Numerous phenomena, such as eclipses and changes in weather, which religion claims are direct acts of God, science explains through the laws of nature. Religion, of course, claims that God wanted it in this way, and the laws of nature exist due to His Grace. Science, on the other hand, does not want to accept the notion of God as it searches for the ultimate theory and the origin of physical laws. Obviously, it is difficult to settle this argument about random vs. divine. What science calls random; religion calls divine.

Regarding the existence of the soul, religion will keep on claiming that it is beyond the realm of science. Science cannot isolate and directly measure certain quantities below a certain magnitude. Religion can always claim that the soul is a subtle field and science does not have the instruments to detect or measure it. Unless science happens to confirm the existence of such a field, the notion of soul and God would remain in the realm of belief and religion and not in science.

- Role of Science & Religion

In my opinion, science and religion are two sides of a coin. Science attempts to understand the mysteries of our universe, whereas religion focuses on understanding the mysteries of life and the notion of 'self'. Science is attempting to explain nature in terms of the laws governing it. However, the deeper it digs into nature, the more mysteries it creates. Quantum mechanics, wave function, relativity, the Standard Model of Particle Physics, and black holes, etc., have created more mysteries, as stated in my next book: Knowing the Unknown Mysteries of The Universe, which need to be resolved.

Let us hope that both religion and science, nevertheless, can learn to coexist. Science has the proper tools and the scientific instruments to open the windows to observe and understand nature. Religion's supernatural explanations, usually based on feelings and faith, are not acceptable to science. Religion should not jump to hasty conclusions just because science has not yet found a rational explanation about certain phenomena. Religion has often done so in the past, and science has then discovered rational explanations for most of the phenomena.

Religion should leave science to unravel the mysteries of the physical world, as science is open to questioning everything including the premises when interpreting data. Religion simply does not want to open its faith and God-based premise to question. Scientists believe that they would eventually discover a theory that would explain everything. It would be quite elegant, sophisticated, and its understanding would require a high degree of intelligence.

When science discovers such a theory, religion could still claim that God was responsible for its Intelligent Design. Religion can thus keep alive the premise that God exists, while science continues to operate successfully with no need for such a premise. Religion can teach

Intelligent Design in theology courses, and science can teach the scientific understanding of the unified theory in science classes.

It will be possible at some point in time for science and religion to come to a common understanding even about the origin and meaning of life. Religion might move away from the obviously false premise regarding the age of the universe and life. Science might come to resolve whether a mysterious force (God), other than the well-known fields, was responsible for causing the Big Bang and for the origin of the universe and life.

Religion might accept some form of subsequent evolution of the universe and life, according to the predefined laws of nature. The cycle of creation, evolution, and destruction might become acceptable to both. The most ancient religion, Hinduism, already accepts this notion.

Nevertheless, the main role of religion should be to encourage the development of 'good' values. This would enable our mind to set more intelligent optimality criteria for further evolution. It would also lead us to become useful members of society, and serve humanity. One's thoughts, emotions, and actions define a person. Religion must teach us to do good, be good and be compassionate. All religions might agree on a common definition of 'good'. Any thought, emotion, or action is good if it helps and does not hurt humankind in any way. Although people might agree with this definition of good and bad, the interpretation of whether they are helping or hurting humankind might be different. Unfortunately, the devil is in the details.

Most religions, directly or indirectly, attempt to modify an individual's values. They focus on improving our values (or stored patterns) in our mind to make us better human beings. As most religions proclaim, our faith should help us improve our values. True faith is not a one-day event, and it must be practiced every moment. What we achieve in our lives follows mostly from our actions, based on the mental analysis of our values. Religion must thus refocus on uplifting humanity to higher planes, closer to God. Scientists should continue seeking answers to the remaining questions.

Unfortunately, our values have not kept pace with the huge amount of information that has become available during the past century. No single individual can use all the information available in different fields. This has led to specialization and less interaction amongst human beings from differing areas of specialization. The exponential rate of growth of knowledge over the last three hundred years would be hard to maintain. Unfortunately, the aggressive instincts that were helpful to cave dwellers for survival have not changed.

Unless we find some means to improve drastically our basic instincts, values, learn to interact, and tolerate each other's point of view; the human race faces the serious danger of becoming extinct. Instead of endlessly arguing about the origin of life, scientists and religious leaders should be more tolerant of each other's views. If we let science continue its mission, we might someday understand how nature works, and religion can still claim that God wanted it to work that way.

Scientists must also realize their responsibility and play carefully with nature. Otherwise, they can cause incalculable sufferings for humanity. A recent development in genetics also has serious implications for humanity. Now that we have mapped the human genome and read the book of DNA, scientists will attempt to rewrite parts of it. At first, we might do so to treat certain diseases, but the temptation of entering self-designed evolution is real; where we change our DNA to improve our physical and mental prowess.

Once we yield to this temptation and attempt to design super humans, they might cause serious problems by subjugating the rest of the humanity. On the other hand, if we did learn to prolong life or develop more-enduring non-biological DNA-based life, we could spread out to other planets in nearby stellar systems. We might run into other intelligent forms of life and settle on other planets.

- Unity in Diversity

Obviously, there cannot be more than one superpower—God. However, all religions can lead to the same destination and all prayers can reach the same God. All religions should lead us to march towards the same destination. There have been great human beings in each religion. They all talked about experiencing God in their lives. Are they all talking about the same God or different Gods? Obviously, one can experience God in many ways and in many forms. According to spiritualists, as our intelligence evolves and we move up in our values, we march towards this supreme intelligence—God.

Unfortunately, most religions do not see this unity in diversity. Each religion has its own image of God. Most of them agree that God is 'He', which is perhaps a reflection of the male dominated society. They simply do not accept that they are talking about the same supreme power. Eastern sages proclaim that just as different people go to the same river via different paths carrying different types of vessels to fetch water, different religions follow different paths using different approaches to seek the same God. Everyone's religion depends on one's birth. A child can be Christian, Hindu or Moslem depending on the faith of the family he or she was born.

The following anecdote illustrates this point. Suppose we are situated on one bank and God is on the other bank of a river. Various boats; representing different religions, are trying to reach the other end. Each boat carries followers of a particular religion. The followers of a particular religion, or people riding in a certain boat, claim that their boat is the only one heading towards the right destination—it has the best route or has a better chance of reaching the destination.

However, nobody knows for sure what is on the other side. People in the other boats should have the freedom to ride in their boats as long as they are not trying to sink the other boats. Unless people in another boat ask for help, we should not impose our will on them. One need not change a boat (religion) in the middle of the stream unless it starts leaking. At the same time, people in different boats (religions) should not try to sink other boats, as long as other boats do not try to sink their boat. Let all religions prosper and help humanity march toward higher goals. Once different religions agree on this concept, the endless fighting will stop.

The United States of America is a great example of unity in diversity, where people from diverse cultures and religion have united and learnt to live in peace and harmony. The United States is a nation of immigrants, immigrants with different religious faiths who have all contributed to the country's prosperity and made it the envy of the entire world.

- Parting Words

When we started our journey, we wanted to answer the following question: Who am I? To answer this question we visited life, as described by genetics, evolution, creation, and religion. We found answers to some but not all the questions. We are still in the middle of the quest for the ultimate truth about the universe and life. Regarding our universe, scientists are making remarkable progress with their experiments, stretching from the tiniest particle to the farthest edges of the universe. However, both scientists and spiritualists are far from discovering the ultimate truth about life, though progress in the field of genetics has been remarkable.

I believe that despite all of the problems in the world, we have a bright future ahead of us. We shall discover many more truths about the universe, life, and religion. Science could one day reveal most of the mysteries of the universe. It could come up with satisfactory answers to the several remaining questions concerning the origin, evolution, and future of the universe and life. Science might have to expand its self-imposed boundaries and go beyond the material world to find the answers.

Science is already extending its boundaries by discovering the scientific meaning of consciousness, which might help science find answer to the question: Who am I? However, we might not find all the answers simply because of our limited intelligence. Nevertheless, we must keep on searching and marching forwards, remembering that the journey itself is an immense source of joy. Our success depends on whether we learn to respect individual freedom, rights, and point of view, appreciate nature and life, and live in peace and harmony.

For religion to have universal appeal, we must agree on certain basic truths. The basic message of all religions is the same, and we must not fight over dogmas that we have created in our respective religions. Obviously, there cannot be more than one God. Call God by any name, but God cannot be partial to or displeased with someone just because that person belongs to a particular religion, race, or gender.

Let religion focus on improving our values, emphasize spirituality, reflect internally on the meaning of life, and explore the truth about the existence of the soul and God, etc. Even if religion insists that God created the universe, we must let scientists have the freedom to look into the mind of God, and discover how God did it. We must realize that science and religion have the same goal—the discovery of the ultimate truth. They should complement each other.

I hope that science and religion might join forces one day. Some day science might also develop tools that enable us to look inwards and analyze our minds. We might then resolve the mystery of life and death, and discover the truth about life, the soul, and even God, although it is unlikely. We might at least be able to set to rest once for all the argument of whether a life force, field, or soul is present in all bodies. Could such a conscious field be part of the supreme force, and if so, could science and religion agree to call this supreme power, God?

Some of us might not accept God as a perceived fact, which according to Vedanta is the only permanent and unchanging force field in this universe. However, all of us can agree that one wastes human life if all one does is dance a little, cry a little, and then die like an animal. One must set high goals, and realize one's true potential. We must attempt to go beyond the mundane pleasures and sorrows of the world and search for perfection, which is unchanging, pure, and absolute bliss. One might not achieve it during one's life, but humanity must march on and the journey must continue until we realize perfection. That is what true religion should mean.

The readers might wonder as to what I truly believe in. Does God exist? As a scientist, all I can say is that I do not know. At the same time, I realize the limitations of my senses and intelligence. Science, at present, cannot prove or disprove the existence of God. Religion draws on God to explain many simple events. Most of them, science can easily explain in terms of the laws of nature. Scientists, on the other hand, with their limited intelligence and experimental tools cannot explain many phenomena including the origin of the fundamental laws of nature.

People, who believe in religion, point to many practices that take our mind away from everyday worldly problems. For example, the practice of meditation, and worship, etc., can bring peace of mind and change our behavior. Fighting the outcome of an action on our part can only bring misery. Scientists might characterize it as control of mind over body and the reprogramming of values in our mind. Science can also explain the feeling of bliss or realizing God through such practices as a state of our mind. Nevertheless, one can exercise remarkable control over the mind and achieve amazing feats. Science has a long way to go to understand the true functioning of our mind and brain.

Nevertheless, none of these points proves or disproves the existence of God. In fact, religion usually defines God as one that is beyond time and space, and not bound to any limitations.

In my opinion, our focus should not be on the question—whether God exists are not. We should instead focus our efforts on how we can lead a better life now that we are here, whether through evolution or creation. Whether one believes in any religion or God, we can be happier if we learn to do our best and not worry about the outcome. All one can do is try harder, and do better next time.

A 'better life' should not mean more wealth or power since many people with such attributes are quite miserable. It should mean whether we are happy, do we have peace of mind, good health, and good values. All of these elements are interdependent. For example, with the right values one derives happiness in helping others and serving humanity. This makes us humble. If the worship of God or practice of meditation—whether due to scientific or religious reasons—brings peace of mind, so be it. After all, it comes down to an individual's faith and belief in God.

While marching on to discover the ultimate truth, let us therefore, learn to respect, and love each other. We must try to see some good in every individual and appreciate the potential divinity in every soul. We should also live in the present and enjoy it. We must stop living in the past, since past is past, and we cannot change it. The future is yet to come. In short, we must learn to live a happy life in the present.

We must take care of our physical, mental, emotional, and spiritual needs. If we fail to take care of even one of these, we will not be happy. For example, if we do not take care of our body and prevent obesity and other health problems, we cannot be happy. Thus, we must control our diet and follow an exercise program. To keep the mind young, we must continue to exercise it by doing crossword puzzles, developing new hobbies, and learning new things. To keep our emotions in check, we must learn to relax. To satisfy our spiritual needs, we must believe in and live by good values. These values include friendship, compassion, detachment, humbleness, non-violence, sacrifice, determination, fearlessness, truth, charity, gentleness, and hatred towards no one. It would certainly make us better human beings.

As I sit in my patio in Oklahoma, hear the thunder of the clouds, and see the rain falling, it strikes me that we are very blessed on our planet Earth. We have the sun; the most important source of energy, water, the atmosphere, the air we breathe, the protective shield around the atmosphere that protects us from harmful radiation, green trees and vegetation, most of the elements including carbon, and different living species.

When we look at the other planets in our solar system, they do not have all these elements of nature. It becomes our responsibility to preserve all of these wonderful elements and not damage the planet and its environment. Nature does its own part by following the physical laws, and we must do our part. We must develop new technology to reduce pollution, put in place some sensible laws, and follow them to preserve our beautiful planet and its environment.

Finally, I believe that the journey through life is similar to traveling by train. The train makes several stops; some passengers get off and others board the train. One day each of us has to get off this train. Therefore, we must strive to make all journeys comfortable and meaningful. .

It has given me great joy writing this book, and I sincerely hope that you, the reader, will also enjoy reading it. *Where am I? How can I control my physical environment?* These questions are investigated in my other two forthcoming books in *Knowing the Unknown* series, *Mysteries of The Universe* and *Challenges of Technology.*

Index

176

Made in the USA
Lexington, KY
18 June 2014